AGAINST ALL ODDS

AGAINST ALL ODDS

Zambia's President Edgar Chagwa
Lungu's Rough Journey to State House

Anthony Mukwita

PARTRIDGE

To order additional copies of this book, contact
Toll Free 0800 990 914 (South Africa)
+44 20 3014 3997 (outside South Africa)
orders.africa@partridgepublishing.com

www.partridgepublishing.com/africa

PREFACE

People write books for many varied reasons but mine was simple.

I lived at a time in the history of Zambia as a writer, when there was not as much interesting literature on our country as perhaps most readers would have preferred there was.

Too little was written about events that shaped the history of our country either in business, religion or politics.

Attending a book event in the Zambian capital, Lusaka at the Taj Pamodzi Hotel just before taking up my mission in Stockholm, Sweden as Deputy Ambassador in March 2015, I was inspired by what President Edgar Chagwa Lungu said in his speech as the chief guest.

The event was in honour of first president of Zambia Kenneth Kaunda's launch of his revised book about the Zambian independence struggle.

During his off the cuff speech, President Edgar Lungu practically threw a gauntlet at Zambian historians and writers to 'go out there and record the history of Zambia so that our children and our children's children can have the luxury of reading our history based on our own historians. Do not wait for people to die before you can document them," he said.

President Lungu might as well have been speaking directly to me because I had already on my computer, a skeleton manuscript on no other than President Edgar Lungu himself regarding the twists of fate that thrust him into the sizzling national political spot-light that thrust him into State House as the sixth president of Zambia.

The words of the celebrated war time British Prime Minister Winston Churchill who said, "history will treat me well. I intend to write it," could have not come more alive to me that day.

I had already collected substantial material on President Edgar Lungu from the time he did pro-bono work for the families of the deceased members of the fateful Gabon air crash that killed all 30 passengers and crew on board in 1993.

My next task then was simple—carefully arrange layer by layer, his life as a politician of humble beginnings and see how this could be turned into material that would add to the body of literature and knowledge in Zambia.

I also sought to debunk the myth that Zambians allegedly have a poor reading culture.

My take on this subject is that 'Zambians have few books to read that are based on successful, tenacious fellow Zambians such as President Edgar Lungu or indeed about extraordinary events in their country as a whole.'

I commenced writing this book in 2014, finally managed to get permission from president Lungu to publish it in August 2016 and found a suitable publisher of high repute at the end 2016.

This is not a book about President Edgar Lungu alone in my considered view. It is a book about African democracy and leadership.

It is a book about Zambia the proverbial last bastion of peace in sub-Saharan Africa and about the great people of the southern African country.

I hope my 'Edgar Lungu story' inspires others to do similar works in order to help show-case our country through literature as we strive to become a relevant part of the global village.

We must tell our own story, our Zambian story because then, and only then can we control it and tell it best and fairly.

Anthony Mukwita.

CONTENTS

'The King is Dead . . .
Long Live the King!'

October 28, 2014, was an exceedingly sad day for all Zambian people, regardless of age, gender, tribe, political, or religious inclination, but particularly so for supporters of the ruling Patriotic Front Party.

The ailing president, the enigmatic, controversial, and widely popular, Michael Chilufya Sata, had just breathed his last in a UK hospital at the age of 77 years. As the news spread, a heavy pall seemed to descend upon the entire nation—the feeling of sadness was palpable.

Just three years into his first five-year term, Michael Sata was still greatly loved and respected. The fact of his progressively failing health had been well known, and public sympathy for both the man and his family was high. To many citizens, Sata embodied fatherliness and the grief was a something personal to them.

In African culture, particularly parts of Southern Africa, leaders wear an aura of omnipresence and intransience, tending to be revered almost to the level of deities—their lofty positions widely assumed to be by divine appointment. They are not expected to die in office. Well, not three years into office at any rate. Therefore, when death does visit high office, as it had just done for the second time in Zambia with Sata's passing, it can be highly devastating. One particularly devastated Zambian was the unassuming Edgar Chagwa Lungu, to whom Michael Sata had been more than a friend and mentor.

Edgar appeared to have had a unique and special place in the heart of the fallen 'king', and was variously, perhaps with more than a touch of envy, referred to as 'the chosen one' or 'the special one' by both friends and foes. By the time of Sata's passing, within the Patriotic Front Party at least (even

1

if not true of the wider public), there certainly was silent acknowledgement of who Lungu was. The implications of this 'specialness', particularly during the final days of President Sata, was not lost on observers.

As expected, messages of condolences and obituaries poured into both the local and international press upon the announcement of Michael Sata's death. In the UK where he died, the newspapers were awash with accounts of how Sata had lived and worked in the UK earlier in his life, driving locomotive trains to and from Victoria Station, among other jobs.

The UK Guardian Newspaper obituary had one of the most interesting summaries of Sata, describing him as 'a charismatic, forceful, but controversial figure', who led the third largest political party to victory in 2011, to become the fifth president of copper-rich Zambia.

Sata's political career stretched all the way back to Zambia's independence with some root hairs said to reach down into the pre-independence era. He had served in various capacities in Kenneth Kaunda's UNIP and Frederick Chiluba's MMD before registering his own Patriotic Front in 2001, and unsuccessfully contesting the presidency the same year, which he did again in 2006 and 2008 (after Mwanawasa's death). Success for Michael Chilufya Sata came by way of an emphatic win over Rupiah Banda's MMD in 2011.

The first president of Zambia was Kenneth Kaunda, president under the United National Independence Party (UNIP) for twenty-seven years from independence in 1964 to 1991. Kaunda was replaced by Frederick Chiluba's Movement for Multiparty Democracy (MMD), which stormed Zambian politics on a platform of 'change': change of national leadership, change from the repressive one-party rule to more representative multiparty politics, and change from overwhelming state control of the economy to economic liberalisation.

The MMD ruled the country for twenty years. Following two five-year terms, Frederick Chiluba, shouted down by all and sundry from an ill-advised attempt at a third term, gave in to pressure to have his party field an alternate candidate. Levy Patrick Mwanawasa of the MMD became the third president of Zambia in 2001 and was re-elected in 2006. In 2008, at the age of fifty-nine, Mwanawasa died in a French hospital, having been evacuated there after suffering a heart attack while attending the African Union (AU) meeting of heads of states in Cairo, Egypt. Former Lusaka governor and diplomat, Rupiah Bwezani Banda (MMD), became

Zambia's fourth president after he was elected to complete Mwanawasa's term; however, he himself lost to the resilient, never-say-die Michael Sata who finally met with success in 2011 in his unrelenting quest for state house.

Sata owed his widely celebrated triumph as much to his indomitable spirit as to a strong and fast-growing support base as voters, disaffected by Banda's reign, deserted the MMD in droves. If such a lengthy chapter on Sata seems like a digression, it is deliberately designed to sketch out the rather outsized shoes that Edgar Chagwa Lungu would be stepping into, as he was thrust into the presidency. Having joined the PF from the United Party for National Development (UPND), Lungu had earned his place in Sata's inner circle as the party's trusty lawyer and one of his confidantes.

On the face of it, the PF's performance in the 2001 elections looked dismal, the party only managing one parliamentary seat, but this was to be expected as they had been legally existent for just one month. Sata's critics called the PF's poll performance a disaster, but not by the calculations of the shrewd 'King Cobra' or 'Mad Mike' to call him by his other moniker. He took the view that being the new kid on the block with little time to campaign and even less by way of financial means, his party, having bagged one parliamentary seat, was a great achievement. This, after all, was more than could be said for a whole lot of parties that had been in existence for much longer with not so much as a councillor to point to.

Buoyed by his first single parliamentary seat, hard won by Emmanuel Mpankata, Sata was almost immediately back on the campaign trail even with the next election a distant five years away. There has probably never been a Zambian politician as focused and flinty in purpose as Sata. In the months that followed, it was evident he had made getting to state house the pursuit of what was left of his political life, and he would not be thwarted by anyone or anything. He was like a dog on a bone.

As a political player, Sata gave as well as he got and was not averse to delivering a low blow. You hit the cobra with a punch, he would come back at you with a stick; you hit him with a stick, and he would come back at you with a political gun. He would keep coming back over and over until one of you was dead—politically, that is. Or maybe even literally, some might argue. He took no hostages.

In the run up to 2006, Sata did two things that left an unfortunate impression on the minds of many people, both locally and internationally. First, he likened the serving president, the staid but likeable Levy Mwanawasa, to a cabbage. He then went on to rip up a real cabbage at a political rally, indicating what he would do to Levy Mwanawasa politically.

The 'vegetable' or 'cabbage' jibe was not new to Levy Mwanawasa's political life. In 1992, while serving as vice-president, he had been injured in a car accident involving the presidential motorcade—no less—which left the once eloquent former solicitor general of Zambia (under Kaunda) with a heavily slurred speech and other injuries.

There was wide debate concerning both his physical and mental health, as to whether Mr Mwanawasa was in any physical or mental shape to withstand the rigours of high office. So unrelenting was the barrage of cabbage jokes in 2001 and beyond that, it remains something of a wonder that Mwanawasa was elected at all. Not once, but twice, for that matter.

The UK Guardian Newspaper described Sata's 2006 cabbage-ripping stunt as cruel and offensive. But if anybody didn't know it by then, this was clear evidence of Michael Sata's ability and willingness to play 'hardball' to carry out a no-holds-barred political campaign style calculated to completely obliterate the opposition that seems to have changed forever the way Zambian politics is played. Sata had just reaffirmed his reputation for political ruthlessness and grotesque insensitivity. He wasn't called 'Mad Mike' or 'King Cobra' for nothing.

In the years between 2006 and 2011, Zambia appeared to have made significant economic gains. Fiscal discipline was evident, the country was on course with its international payments, the donor community was happy, and investors were beating a path to Zambia, bringing with them much needed Foreign Direct Investment or FDI.

Unfortunately, in spite of the favourable economic indicators, the fact was that the majority of the country's citizens were poor, with many unemployed and more than 50 per cent living below internationally approved measures of poverty. The country was also rocked by rumours of corruption in high places, officialdom was largely perceived as being less than transparent, and people close to the government were constantly in the news for one alleged corrupt act or another.

In addition, there were murmurs of discontent relating to the sale of major mining firms with the enduring view among many that the family silver had been disposed of too cheaply (by the MMD), denying the country its proper dues from its vast mineral wealth.

It only added to the sense of frustration that a number of mines had been sold to various investors, including Chinese investors, who were making headlines for their shabby treatment of local workers and seemingly getting away with it.

Following economic liberalisation, the new capitalist owners of industry in Zambia had discovered a novel way to cut labour costs (apart from simply cutting jobs)—casualization of the labour force—to the extent where in some mines, up to 90 per cent of workers were employed in non-permanent, low-paid roles.

This phenomenon cut across all major industries including mining, construction, and manufacturing. The result was that out of desperation, thousands of once proud and dignified employed individuals were reduced to scrambling for few available jobs and accepting to work under less than favourable terms. Amid public perception that the MMD Government was doing nothing to address peoples' concerns, the murmurs of discontent continued to grow louder by the day, and it was not long before 'change' became the rallying cry of the next presidential election campaign. Any candidate to promise that was sure to win.

Shrewd politician that he was, Michael Sata took full advantage of the widespread disgruntlement, launching an aggressive populist campaign against the MMD and its government. His denunciation speeches, delivered mainly via recorded radio interviews and at well-attended rallies, resonated deeply with a cross-section of society, including academics, professionals, but especially with the many low-income earners engaged in a perpetual struggle to hold body and soul together.

Evidence that Sata's promise of change was hitting home could be seen in the rate at which his diatribes were recorded, uploaded, quoted, and shared via social media by a very diverse audience. They were even being sold on the streets. The King Cobra was fast becoming a cult figure.

When not railing directly at the MMD, Sata seemed to direct a particularly nasty venom at Chinese investors. Not believing that they were adding any real value to the Zambian economy, he called them 'infestors'.

Some of his most scathing attacks, leading up to 2011, were reserved for Chinese owners of mining and construction companies. They, themselves, did not help diplomatic matters much, as they were regularly in the news accused of gross human rights and worker abuse, underpaying their employees, and casualising just about every job they were willing to offer to Zambians.

Sata saw this as a clear disrespect for the Zambian Government and took particular offence. In his usual abrasive manner, Sata touched on a particularly sensitive part of China's political anatomy, threatening to recognise Taiwan, the East Asian island country over which Beijing still claims sovereignty as an independent state and establish diplomatic relations with it. That would almost certainly have led to the severing of some fifty years' worth of trade and diplomatic ties between Lusaka and Beijing.

How China would feed its insatiable appetite for Zambian copper and how, on the other hand, Zambia would survive an economic future without the massive benefits of its economic relations with Beijing is hard to imagine under such a scenario. Thankfully, Zambians never got to find out because when Sata did become president after the 11 September 2011 poll, he surprised everyone by extending an olive branch to the Chinese Government as one of the first pieces of business. His Taiwan agenda had, for the time being, been shelved, it seemed.

This may have been one of the first signs of the unpredictability of Michael Sata's presidency and character, but it was definitely not his last. Throughout his short tenure, it was the one word by which his reign could best be described. Like him or not, in the three short years before his death, President Sata managed to carve an indelible mark on infrastructure development in the country, for which he will be warmly be remembered for years to come.

Doubtless, some projects dated back to the Mwanawasa presidency, and were handed down through the Rupiah Banda (MMD) administration to the PF. However, there were others, notably the tarring of long kilometres of township roads, a couple of major bridges, and a university in the Northern Province of Zambia, which were initiated by the PF on an understanding that all provinces of Zambia would have themselves at least one government university. There was also progress in the form of the upgrading of several colleges to universities, and completion of the new

Levy Mwanawasa General Hospital in Lusaka. Sata had commenced on ambitious plans to build roads, bridges, and universities from the day he was sworn into office as part of his plan to create jobs and reduce poverty.

Sata's ruthless approach in dealing with foes, both real and perceived, was legendary; he was, after all, the King Cobra, and you crossed his path at your own peril. However, in spite of the rough exterior, those who knew him or worked closely with him swore to God that he was one of kindest men they had ever encountered. It is said that he snarled at people only to protect himself from manipulation, but was in fact a man with a very soft core, often going out of his way to render generous support to those in need. Such was the paradoxical nature of the man. It is not clear how men like Michael Sata are made, but one thing is for sure; they are a once in a lifetime occurrence—a hard act to follow.

It seems like Edgar has his work cut out. To quote a really tired cliché, the journey that Edgar has embarked on is definitely not for the faint-hearted. It has 'Welcome to the school of hard-knocks' written all over it. Edgar Lungu would now, or eventually, need to step out of Michael Sata's shadow and show the nation what he's got. Edgar Lungu restated that he was 'up to the task.'

With his re-election on 11 August 2016, declaration as winner on 15 August and subsequent inauguration on 13 September 2016, Edgar Chagwa Lungu has at least the next five years to design his own footprint on Zambia's history. What will he be remembered for when the history of Zambia is written?

THE CANDIDATE AND
HIS 'FRENEMIES'

That Zambians are hard core political animals, evidenced by the buzz of excitement that often lights them up ahead of an election, whether at presidential or parliamentary level. It may be some form of overcompensation for almost three decades of one-party rule, but Zambians seem to enjoy nothing better than a good old fashioned high-stakes winner-takes-it-all contest, such as a snap presidential election caused by an unfortunate death in state house, as the case was in 2008 when President Levy Patrick Mwanawasa passed on, and in 2014 when President Michael Chilufya Sata died.

In terms of excitement, the 2014 election that elevated Lungu from a mere cabinet minister to president of Zambia ran true to tradition. There was one big difference, though—the political dynamics at play following the death of President Sata and their influence in defining his successor as party leader and as republican president if the PF was to fend off the opposition.

It is these dynamics that made Lungu's journey to the presidency perhaps the most interesting of all, and the election itself one of the most riveting to follow in the history of Zambian politics. The twists and turns abound. The pre-election period was fast-paced, fluid and ever so unpredictable, not to mention the emotional and financial cost it exacted on the party and its leadership.

No one could tell today what would happen tomorrow. In fact, it was hard enough just to predict what might happen in the very next hour, as the party's leadership, still badly shaken by the passing of Sata and fractured by a vicious succession war, tried to come to terms with their massive, unexpected loss.

This state of flux would continue until the very last day that Lungu would be sworn into the office of president. Lungu had but twenty-one days to campaign for the most coveted job in town compared to his main rival, Hakainde Hichilema, who had already taken four shots at the presidency but lost.

The highs and lows seemed to run ad infinitum, threatening to imperil the party's very existence, not to mention its chances at the coming election. Guy Scott, the estranged vice-president of the ruling party and now opposition UPND overt supporter, did not help matters. If anything, he seemed hell-bent on grinding Lungu to the ground.

Perhaps a little peek into Zambia's democratic history and process of polls might give more perspective and help clear the grey areas being discussed here: the intricacies that made Lungu's election arguably the most keenly followed poll since Zambia started keeping political records, and perhaps the most hardest won fight by any single politician.

Dr Kenneth David Kaunda became the leader of post–independence Zambia; first, as prime minister for several months running up to independence in 1964, and then as president between 1972 and 1991 when UNIP was the only political party allowed to exist. Kaunda called his invention a 'one-party participatory democracy'. Who does that? Anyhow, under this model, every Zambian that's qualified to vote was invited to participate in elections held every five years on the UNIP ticket with the unwritten rule that citizens could challenge for any elective post, except that held by the man himself.

A few political daredevils did try and suffice to say it did not end very well for them. Kaunda, always the sole candidate on the presidential ballot, won every poll in clockwork fashion, remaining the leader of Zambia for as long as Nelson Mandela was a political prisoner under apartheid South Africa—twenty-seven years. But like the adage goes, 'nothing lasts forever'. Kaunda was shunted out of state house by a landslide victory for the MMD in 1991 that marked a return to multiparty politics in Zambia.

Frederick Titus Jacob Chiluba, the new big small man in the big house, had to deal with challenges to his reign posed by ex-MMD comrades like

Ben Y. Mwila, Dean Mungo'mba, and General Christon Tembo, as well as the formidable Anderson Mazoka who had gone on to found the UPND.

President Chiluba stepped down in 2001 due to a constitutional clause that restricted presidential tenure to two five-year terms. Needless to say, the late president had allowed an acrimonious public discussion to be held regarding a possibility of changing the constitution to allow a third five-year term beyond the constitutionally embedded two five-year term restriction. These attempts, which President Chiluba publicly said he had nothing to do with, were vehemently thwarted and never saw the light the day. To date, a Zambia president can only run for two five-year terms. In the case of President Edgar Lungu, however, the two five year term clause did not apply because he had served less than two and half years in office after he replaced the late President Sata. Lawyers maintained as a matter of fact that he was legible to run in 2021 again because his first full five year term only commenced in 2016.

Chiluba's attempt at a third term was inspired in part by a cabal of twenty-two Pentecostal preachers from the Copperbelt who claimed it was the will of God for the bible-quoting, tongue-speaking Chiluba to stay an extra five years in office in order to complete his God-given duty. Fortunately, he had the good sense to walk away following widespread and shrill condemnation of his machinations including a loss of a life.

FTJ, as a section of the media loved to call him, would live out the rest of his life shuttling between his home and the courthouse, as he battled a raft of graft allegations arising from his time in office. When he wasn't in either of the two places, the man, who had presided over the fastest economic liberalisation programme in Africa, was lying in a hospital bed in South Africa receiving treatment for a debilitating heart condition.

FTJ's successor, Levy Patrick Mwanawasa, could not have started off on a more challenging note when he won the 2001 polls. The election had delivered a hung parliament, comprising more opposition lawmakers than legislators from his own party the MMD, a party he had once ditched after accusing Chiluba of being too soft on graft.

In vying for the top job in 2001, Mwanawasa had scored a paltry 29.6 per cent of the entire presidential vote cast in that election. In other words, more people voted for other candidates put together than they did for him. However, constitutionally at least, this did not disqualify Mwanawasa, as at the time, Zambia employed the 'first past the post' or 'simple majority' model of deciding presidential polls. Doubtless, this model was highly unrepresentative and not without controversy. The demure Mwanawasa became the third president of Zambia amid protests from both within and without his own party, with many challenging the legitimacy of his election.

However, lacking constitutional backing and with only half-hearted public support, the protests soon died down. Mazoka of the UPND, the other contender for the presidency (who was, it was rumoured, had been robbed of victory in the 2001 poll), had in the meantime succumbed to poor health, thus easing some of the pressure off Mwanawasa.

Sata, forced to leave the MMD because being sidelined for the top job by Chiluba in favour of Mwanawasa, performed dismally. By the next round of polls in 2006, Mwanawasa had proved himself to be not only an astute and formidable player but a player to contend with. His refusal to be a Chiluba puppet doubtless won him substantial respect and the much needed support.

It was on Mwanawasa's watch that the 'presidential immunity law' that shields former presidents from prosecution had been lifted by parliament in a move unprecedented in Zambian history to pave way for Chiluba's prosecution on a number of corruption charges. Mwanawasa's 'zero tolerance for corruption' stance was music to many Zambian peoples' ears, especially the poor, and he won the 2006 election with a more substantial vote.

In 2008, Rupiah Bwezani Banda, a football and boxing-loving former diplomat and ex-governor of the city of Lusaka, was called out of retirement from his village in Chipata to serve as vice president to Mwanawasa following a sudden vacancy in the vice president's office. Mr Banda could most certainly claim to have had the easiest ride of all to the presidency as the man on hand upon the death of Mwanawasa. Analysts say Banda was brought in as a 'compromise' and 'safe' vice president from his retirement sanctuary in Chipata, Eastern Province, near the border with Malawi, to deputise for a president who would die months later.

Before Banda, the office was held by the colourful and dapper fire and brimstone preaching, Reverend Nevers Mumba, who was fired for what many saw as a breach of 'Cardinal Law of Power Number 48': 'never try to outshine the master'. Doing so can prove to be a deadly sin, as Pastor Mumba soon found out.

Banda stepped up to the plate upon President Mwanawasa's unfortunate but not very surprising demise in 2008. Mwanawasa had already suffered at least one major stroke and had historical health issues contributing to fast physical deterioration. Capitalising on an obvious 'sympathy vote' in a snap presidential by-election, Banda managed to keep out both Sata of the PF and the young and hungry upstart, Hichilema of the UPND, to become the fourth president of Zambia.

However, even then Sata must have sensed that his long wait for the big job could not be that far from the end. 'Mr Banda is going to go down in history as the shortest serving President of Zambia,' Sata repeatedly told his supporters as he hit the hustings for the 2011 elections employing all the tactics he had rehearsed in previous failed attempts.

With almost military precision, Sata dismantled the MMD and President Banda, taking the ruling party apart piece by piece with the help of foot soldiers such as Edgar Lungu and Guy Scott.

In Zambian presidential elections, there is usually a common factor where you have one ruling party candidate facing one strong opposition candidate, plus a number of sideshow candidates, much like a heavyweight boxing contest supported by a number of undercard bouts. And so it was in 2011 that there were many small opposition candidates whose role, it seemed, was to make up the numbers on the ballot paper and to add colour and flavour to the real poll.

Some, like Chama Chakomboka (during FTJ's time), Muliokela, and Dr Cosmo Mumba, more recently have proved their own value in other ways by supplying some much-needed comic relief to an event that can be a bloody affair in a very literal sense. Sata did have a sense of humour, one of the most potent crowd-pulling weapons he possessed, even if he sometimes took things a little too far.

In 2011, he was the strong opposition candidate. Having contested and lost three times previously, he was still the underdog; just this time, a much more experienced and dangerous one. Like the biblical David, not only did he bring down the Goliath that was Rupiah Banda, it would seem, from the MMD's inexorable slide into oblivion since that defeat, that the political giant had also had its head cut off. With the MMD in terminal decline, it was hard to imagine that in the 2015 presidential poll occasioned by Sata's death, the man widely regarded as his chosen successor, Edgar Lungu, would have to battle anyone else other than the UPND's Hichilema who was becoming something of a serial contender.

That analysis was proved wrong even before Sata had been put to rest. It turned out there were quite a few others among Lungu's cabinet colleagues and fellow members of the PF hierarchy who had their own designs on State House.

In ordinary times, many of the candidates, now putting themselves forward, would be hard to sell outside the PF even with the party's machinery behind them, but these were special circumstances and seemingly free pass to the presidency seemed touch of a frenzy of interest. Where were they getting the courage and inspiration from? It was not long before the finger of suspicion fell on Guy Scott, the acting president. Scott had been a faithful lieutenant and close friend of Michael Sata's—his alter ego for years. Or so it seemed on paper.

Like devoted, indefatigable missionaries, the two had traversed the length and breadth of Zambia, taking the PF gospel of 'lower taxes and more money in your pockets' from village to village. Scott's loyalty to Sata was ostensibly unquestionable.

A first-generation descendant of Scottish settlers, Scott himself was barred from standing for the highest office in the land by the 'Parentage Clause' of the Zambian Constitution. Not that it mattered much, as it is unlikely that enough Zambians, even five decades after colonial rule, would vote for a white man to win the presidency—even one who, owing to his age, had been a 'Zambian' citizen longer than many of the electorate.

Guy Scott would be accused of playing what some have called the most 'divisive' role in Zambian ruling party politics until 26 January 2015 when he declined a lower cabinet post offered to him by Lungu. Guy Scott's role in the events leading up to 25 January 2015 is discussed a little later in the book.

For now, perhaps a little step back so as to examine the factors that made the Lungu rise to high office different from others before him, both at party and national level.

President Edgar Chagwa Lungu salutes the gathered crowd at Heroes National Stadium on 13th September 2016 after being re-elected with more than 50 percent of the total votes cast in the 11th August 2016 crucial poll.

President Edgar Lungu is driven back to State House in an armoured Presidential car after inauguration at National Heroes Stadium on 13th September 2016.

Commander-in-Chief of all armed forces in Zambia President Edgar Lungu with Zambia Army Commander Lt. General Paul Mihova. President Lungu and General Mihova attended the same prestigious Officers military School in the Central Province of Zambia, Military Establishment of Zambia or MILTEZ.

Before his death on 28 October 2014, Sata, in the eyes of many Zambians, did everything he could to show, short of a public anointing ceremony, that he favoured Edgar Lungu as his preferred successor were anything to happen to him. Before his departure for London in October 2014, for what should have been a routine medical check-up, the president did two significant things. First, he sacked Wynter Kabimba who, until his spectacular fall from grace was the almighty secretary general of the ruling Patriotic Front party, and the country's Minister of Justice, both roles terminated on 28 August 2014.

To say Kabimba was a powerful figure in the PF is an understatement. Much has been said about his ability to change people's lives (usually for the worst) at the click of his fingers. It has also been said, with alarming seriousness, that 'seas would part' when he gave the word.

How Kabimba came to be this powerful is a bit of a mystery, for he had never won an election, and could therefore not boast any constituency, neither was he especially favoured of Sata. Plainly put, there were more in and outside the party that disliked him than those who did, and the event of his political crash-landing appeared to have been an event of much joy. So spontaneous and so intense was the jubilation at Kabimba's fall from grace that more than a little malice could be suspected. People were literally congratulating Sata for still having enough 'venom' in him to carry out this act. The German word *Schadenfreude* seemed to have been invented for just this occasion. Why such universal glee at one man's misfortune is perhaps a topic for another book on Zambian politics. For now, we turn back to Edgar Lungu.

Sata's next significant act before his fateful trip to the London hospital was to insert yet more feathers into Edgar Lungu's cap; everything he took away from Wynter Kabimba, he bestowed on Lungu.

And so Lungu became the most titled man in Sata's cabinet, adding the portfolio of Minister of Justice, and the powerful position of secretary general of the PF to those he already held as Minister of Defence, as well as chairperson of the disciplinary committee of the ruling party.

When it came time to leave for London, President Sata looked around for his favourite and heir-apparent. Upon being informed that Edgar had, earlier that day, been sent to Luanda, Angola to represent Zambia at a SADC Heads of States Summit, Sata ordered his immediate return back home. He was not about to hand over the 'instruments of power' to anyone else in his cabinet despite having a whole cadre of capable ministers to choose from.

No one can say for sure what the president's state of mind was shortly before he left for the United Kingdom, but one thing for sure is that he had decided exactly whom he wanted to leave in charge of the affairs of the state in his absence, and he would not be dissuaded.

As Lungu recalls, 'We had just arrived in Angola, and I was being told that the president wanted me back. It was a very unsettling moment because I did not know what that meant. It could have meant I was being fired or something else. I had no way of telling what was happening because you cannot really second guess a presidential decision, especially if that president is Sata.'

Lungu flew back to Lusaka, and in the middle of the night, not long before Sata's departure for London at about 1.00 a.m. and found himself in the role of acting president. When the instruments of power were bestowed on Lungu on that occasion, he'd had the presence of mind to thank the president for the gesture, saying, 'Not only am I humbled and grateful to President Sata for the show of confidence. I am equal to the task, and shall not disappoint him as I dispense my duties as acting president of Zambia. I am really grateful to President Sata.' Ominous words, considering what was to come in the not too distant future.

Michael Sata was accompanied on his last earthly journey by wife, Dr Christine Kaseba Sata, and oldest son, Mulenga, who at the time held the post of Mayor of Lusaka. Sata would be hospitalised in London for two weeks, his family being supported at the bedside by embassy officials like acting Deputy High Commissioner, Amos Chanda, and others.

In the meantime, Lungu continued in his stand-in role with the 'cooperation' of his party colleagues, as well as the security wings. After all, the president had left the country in the past, and had returned.

In private, however, Lungu, knowing how gravely ill his boss was, would confess to confidantes when prodded how he and his wife, Esther, prayed fervently for Sata's recovery and safe return home. This was not some power-hungry prince secretly rubbing his hands in glee with his eye on the ticking clock. He was happy enough with his pouchful of portfolios.

This humility might explain why Sata felt so safe leaving Lungu in charge, for with it, too, comes a mark of leadership.

On 24 October 2014, Lungu led the annual Independence Day celebrations at the newly constructed National Heroes' Stadium in Lusaka, this time round to mark fifty years of self-rule—the so-called jubilee.

It was a historic event and heads of state from across Africa were in attendance or had sent representatives. Zambia, as usual, was heralded as a beacon of peace. An orderly nation, which had made significant economic gains in the recent past, and an example for the rest of the continent. In American parlance, the country was on a 'home run' of peace and stability on a continent where turbulence was more the norm.

Little did the jubilating nation and its visitors know what unpleasant news awaited just around the corner. In an eerie foretaste of events to come in just a few days, the army brass band at the stadium played sombre music, and then shot off a twenty-one-gun salute as a tribute to the ailing, absent president. Four days later, Lungu got a call in the dead of night informing him that the president was no more.

The announcement of Sata's death changed Lungu's life forever. Even though he was a cabinet minister several degrees higher than the others, the passing of Sata put him in contention for the highest office in the land, which apart from a death in State House, might still have remained no more than a remote possibility for him.

As the awful news of Sata's passing was carried on the airwaves and official channels, the acting president's home became the focal point of grief, the 'funeral house', to borrow a Zambian term, where mourners and well-wishers gathered to express their grief, and pay their respects to the departed.

Following a telephone alert from London to be at Lungu's side, this author was the first person to get there, as people started to arrive at the 'Lungus' home just after midnight.

A caucus was planned for the next morning at six o'clock to be attended by cabinet ministers and chaired by Lungu in order to determine the way forward. When would Sata's body be brought back home, official announcements of his death, etc., to quell overnight speculation.

Emmanuel Mwamba, Kelvin Bwalya Fube, Kaizar Zulu later arrived at the Lungu house to help boost plans for the caucus, but met great resistance from some ministers who said the attempts to perpetuate Lungu's stay in office as acting president were not only 'illegal', but could be tantamount to treason.

'Lungu is not the acting president Mwamba and you Kaiza. It is Guy Scott who is the acting president,' one top official from the ministry of foreign affairs said ferociously.

The scary word treason started flying around a lot in the morning of Sata's death, as it was repeated later by then Attorney General Musa Mwenye and a top ranking official from the office of the secretary to the cabinet. They were all vehemently and openly opposed to Lungu's continued stay in office for reasons best known to themselves.

The acting president did not have the luxury to sit down and cry or mourn. Such a whirlwind of events followed, and it was hard to keep pace. Firstly, there was a hasty transfer of power to the designated vice president, Guy Scott.

Even though Lungu had been left in charge, his mandate, according to the law, was valid only for as long as the substantive holder of the office was still alive and able to delegate.

Sections of the national constitution required that in the event of the death of a serving president, the vice president at the time is to take over the reins of power for ninety days, after which elections would be held for citizens to choose a new president. This scenario was not without precedent in Zambia. It had happened in 2008 when Mwanawasa died in office. The only difference was that when Mwanawasa left the country on that fated trip, the man in whom he left the instruments of power as acting president and vice president had been one and the same person.

Guy Scott became acting president after the short-lived Attorney General Musa Mwenye cited some laws to make Scott assume power despite there having been no vacancy, as the position of acting president was already held by Edgar Lungu. The initially quiet forces against Lungu suddenly reared their ugly heads up. And they were many.

The power transfer was done to the clear dismay of majority cabinet ministers, Members of the Central Committee (MCC) of the ruling PF and councilors countrywide that had already recognised Lungu as the heir apparent. These felt that there was no need to change leadership. After all, Lungu had held the ship together so well thus far.

Lungu, remaining as acting president of Zambia until elections in ninety days, would have observed the 'spirit' of the law, or, at any rate, required a speedy amendment of the law that would have prevented him from doing so in the interest of stability.

However, the then attorney general, Musa Mwenye, decided on observance of the 'letter' of another law, in his endeavour to uphold the supreme law of the land. The devil was in the detail.

Of course, this decision played very well into the camp of those who did not support Lungu's bid for the presidency, and hoped they had been brought closer to getting rid of him. The merits or demerits of both sides of the constitutional argument will probably be the subject of legal debate in Zambia for many years to come. Suffice it to say that that decision might have contributed to Musa Mwenye's very short tenure as the country's attorney general. He did not survive the first ninety days of Edgar Lungu's presidency.

The same morning, early after President Sata's passing, Edgar Lungu received an intelligence brief about the change of power that was to take place, according to the attorney general's directive, which he agreed to.

Words like 'treason' were yet again cast around to scare anyone that supported Lungu from backing him. No one wanted to go to jail this morning or another.

Protests, at this development, came mainly from the 'supporting' cabinet ministers who had gathered at Lungu's house, including Prof Nkandu Luo (Chiefs and Traditional Affairs Minister), Jean Kapata (Tourism Minister), and Ngosa Simbyakula (Home Affairs Minister), lawyers Kelvin Bwalya Fube, stalwarts like the late Willie Nsanda, Kaizar Zulu and Emmanuel Mwamba including Emmanuel Chilubanama. The mood was tense, as alliances within the PF began to take shape.

In the meantime, Edgar Lungu had donned a smart black round-collar Asian style [mourning] suit for the mourning period. He looked tired and drained, probably from the events leading up to the twenty-eight of October, but very likely due to the fact that he was carrying on his shoulders the hopes and aspirations of dozens of his friends and supporters, while no doubt dealing with the antagonism of those not in his camp, not to mention the fence-sitters. Lungu's eyes were slowly opening up to many political realities.

On the morning of 29 October 2014, Lungu was a shadow of his usual youthful energetic confident self as he walked to the parked presidential motorcade that would drive him to state house to hand over the instruments of power to the vice president, Guy Scott.

Lungu was literally giving up the power handed to him by his friend, mentor, and now departed boss, Michael Sata. Ironically, the power handover was to a man whose rank Sata had hardly given public recognition.

In that instant, Lungu must have known something that not too many people did. He was ready to fight another day on his own terms, but just not today. He remains unequivocal today that handing over the instruments of power without resistance was the best thing under the circumstances even if some people might have seen it as a cowardly act. Lungu was only looking out for the interests of the nation he loved, and was doing his best to ensure the peace and political stability of the country. This was important to him.

Lungu did not believe in expending his entire arsenal on a small war or killing a fly using a sledgehammer. He is a meticulous and calculating soldier and lawyer. It was hard to see him coming, but that was always his secret weapon. You never saw him coming, and you often did not see him for a politician.

A well-known latent quotematic, also being a learned member of the bench, as well as a natural orator, Lungu, citing his favourite book, the Bible, told journalists in Lusaka ahead of President Sata's burial that he was no 'megalomaniac'.

Lungu's decision to handing over power to Scott served to endear him much to the public, but perhaps more usefully to the press. Scott, on the other hand, quickly began to look like the power-hungry politician; one who was trying to undermine the express wishes of his departed friend.

Meanwhile, Lungu remained calm, almost like playing to the gallery, much to the delight of a controversy-hungry press and resentment of his foes who wished him away. When it was his turn to pay his respects to Sata, whose body was lying in state at the Mulungushi International Conference Centre in Lusaka, Lungu cited his concern for the nation's stability as the reason why he had handed over power to Scott so easily, thereby possibly putting himself out of contention for the presidential race.

Narrating the famous biblical example of King Solomon's wisdom, Lungu said, 'You see, King Solomon, a very wise leader, was encountered by two women. They were each claiming that one child was their own. As the tensions rose, King Solomon asked for a sword so that he could split the child in two parts and give the women a half of the child each. At that point, the real mother begged King Solomon to give the baby to the other woman in order to save it.'

Lungu continued, 'This is just an example of where we are now. I love the people of Zambia just like Mr Sata did. I, therefore, wouldn't want to risk the peace we enjoy by holding on to power. If power is in the wrong hands now, so be it. It is (in wrong hands) only for ninety days after all.'

That single statement, it would seem, catapulted Lungu's campaign miles further than those of his opponents. More statements were to come. Lungu went further to explain how politics, the law and power, (ought to) play out in situations where a president has died, to the journalists. 'We (Zambia) have two centres of power. One under Article 38 of the Constitution and the other under Article 39 (1), which I was appointed under. I, instead, chose the interest of the Zambian people, the safety, peace, and good order. I gave it (power) away for peace.'

As the journalists furiously scribbled down his comments, Lungu explained that Zambia needed to have a unified command under one commander-in-chief of the armed forces. He was proving to be a real chess player.

'Suppose I had my own power centre and there were forces putting their weight behind me and the other guy did not have it, what would have happened?' Lungu asked like a college professor prodding his students for answers to a complicated problem. What Lungu was explaining is that jostling for power would have easily thrust Zambia into a deep sea of instability that could have been hard to navigate out of. Lives would have been possibly lost needlessly, and Lungu wanted not blood on his hands.

Just when they thought they had heard enough, he carried on, 'We all rallied behind him (President Sata), he formed this party (PF), and we joined, so at the end of the day, we should ensure his vision lives on. We should choose the best person to carry his vision.' Lungu continued, 'We were all students of Mr Sata. We bought into his vision, and that is why we are confident we will carry on from where he left off.'

As a parting shot, he asked the media to help caution members of his party to bring to an end succession talks that risked deepening divisions, and focus instead on giving the 'old man' a funeral worthy of his status in the party and nation. 'This is not time to talk about power and transition. It is time to mourn and respect our leader,' Lungu stressed.

Lungu also repeated he was not at all worried about who would take over from President Sata. It appeared he was ruling himself out of the race. Even so, his actions and pronouncements were already helping to project him as a top contender, a General in the making, the Big Kahuna.

In the days that would follow, and while thousands of Zambians continued to troop to the Mulungushi Conference Centre to pay their last respects to Sata, the battle lines were being drawn for the start of Zambia's own 'rumble in the jungle'. In a move unprecedented since the return to multiparty politics in Zambia, the ruling party had a record of eleven candidates, among them members of the Sata family, all vying to replace him.

In the race were Sata's widow, Dr Christine Kaseba, his nephew, Miles Sampa, and in-law, Bob Sichinga. Others were Geoffrey Bwalya Mwamba (MP and controversial businessman popularly known as G. B. M.), MP for Kabwata Given Lubinda, MP for Nchanga Central Wylbur Simuusa, MP for Bwana Mkubwa, Emmanuel Chenda, retired army officer and former diplomat, Captain Selemani Phangula, and Chishimba Kambwili, MP for Luanshya.

If he were harbouring any secret ambitions of contesting the presidency himself, Lungu now had a very good idea of the ominous forces arrayed against him that he would have to contend with certainly nothing he would have bargained for.

To say it was a politically messy affair is putting it mildly. However, the debacle worked to Lungu's advantage, as he looked increasingly like the victim of a conspiracy, and he would have calculated that were the ten to rally behind one contender, they might have a better chance of stopping him. Divided, his chances of success would be fairly high, especially with the public's sympathy appearing to in his favour.

As the battle within the PF raged, Edgar Lungu, still playing the reluctant heir, began to emerge more and more as the man of the moment. Guy Scott, Lungu's nemesis, was at this point in the role of referee. Using his considerable power and resources as acting president, Scott held on until 18 November to announce a date for the presidential by-election, 20 January 2015.

In referring to the twentieth of January poll, Scott stated, 'As acting president, I want to leave a legacy of peaceful and fair elections,' Scott told reporters after leading his cabinet ministers in signing the books of condolences at his official residence in Lusaka in honour of the late Sata.

However, by now, an obvious bias on Scott's part was evident against Lungu's candidacy. Short of openly and publicly denouncing him, Scott made it crystal clear that he preferred, and would throw his weight in support of, any candidate other than Lungu.

His open contempt for Edgar Lungu, who had once served as a Deputy Minister in Scott's office was unmistakable as it was palpable. However, perhaps the contempt was mutual, as Lungu, it seemed, did not miss any opportunity to spite Scott back, totally out of character though.

'It would be unacceptable for anyone to start campaigning for the forthcoming presidential by-election for themselves and indeed on behalf of someone else,' Scott said as the nation continued to mourn Sata. 'Police will be alert to deal with anyone involved in illegal activities,' Scott said, clearly flexing his political muscle, and sending a signal to the police for quick action.

More will follow in subsequent chapters on Guy Scott's efforts to de-campaign Lungu. Let's just say for now that, at this point, many had begun to wonder who Guy Scott really was, and why he seemed so dead set against Lungu? Could it be there was more to all this maneuvering than met the eye?

And What's with the Guy?

As the 'civil war' within the PF raged on, local and foreign media were working overtime, trying to dissect the multiple layers that made up the political players in the race, bit by bit, and laying them bare for the Zambian public to chew on as much as possible. Time, of course, was waiting for no one.

In one such instance, the UK Telegraph attempted to unravel the myth that was Guy Scott, whom they described as a 70-year-old Cambridge-educated economist. Many Zambians were already aware of who Scott was, having played a big role in the MMD's rise to power that finally ended the seemingly invincible UNIP's 27-year vice-like grip on Zambian politics back in 1991.

To the average Zambian, he was the avuncular white man who wowed the crowds with his withering put-downs of rival politicians, the comments often delivered in the local language.

In The Telegraph story, Scott had proudly described himself as 'a white Zambian, but not representing white interests'. Former United States President, George W Bush, when he visited Zambia on one of his two charity trips to the southern African country, had lightly referred to Guy as 'a scaly, ol' dude', while the Zambian opposition liked to refer to him as a 'stupid white old man' (a description first attributed to Hakainde Hichilema, who later became his best buddy when Scott decamped the PF to campaign against Lungu in the August 2016 general elections) who now, in his acting role, stood as Africa's only white president, years after colonialism was discarded. Zambia's white president, just weeks after celebrating fifty years of independence (Jubilee) from colonial rule, sounded like an oxymoron in the eyes and ears of the cynics.

Scott shot to international stardom when President Sata made him the first white vice president of post–independence Zambia after bagging the 11 September 2011 poll. Before that, he had stolen the local media limelight for ordering the killing of hundreds of Zambian pigs suspected to have contracted the swine flu, as Minister of Agriculture under FJT. Among the herds slaughtered were some animals belonging Scott himself. Many questions surrounded that 'massacre' in local media, but with time, as with so many other things, they fizzled out.

President Sata and Scott had been old political allies and 'firm' friends as The Telegraph quickly pointed out in their interview with him. The newspaper added that Guy was aware of the consternation and deep discomfort his appointment caused to some people. That even race was unwittingly read into it, a white vice president, years after independence from colonial Britain.

Although a vast majority of Zambians would normally describe themselves as being as aracial, as they are non-tribal, for quite a number of them, the picture did not quite fit.

Sata, though, had evidently thought nothing of his buddy's skin colour. 'I don't think Michael thought it was a racial thing. He just thought it was a good idea,' Scott told The Telegraph during an interview in 2012. 'I have been involved in politics here for a long time. As a schoolboy, I was involved in the liberation movement.' Scott fondly recalled how he attracted surprise at public functions when, 'You see people's jaws drop. They think there's been a mistake with the seating plan or something. A white Zambian, but not representing white interests, that's the point.'

He was born in Livingstone. His father had emigrated to what was then the British Protectorate of Northern Rhodesia in 1927 where he worked as a doctor, a politician, a lawyer, and a newspaper editor at what is now known as the Zambia Daily Mail.

Scott returned to Britain to study mathematics and economics at Trinity Hall, Cambridge. He later took a doctorate in cognitive science from Sussex University and lectured in robotics at Oxford. Like the late President Sata, Scott had been dogged by rumours of ill-health including one suggesting that he was suffering from advanced Parkinson's disease that caused the involuntary shaking of one hand (others said alcohol made the hand shake). Not that Zambians cared at all, as they had already proved in electing Mwanawasa and Sata, both whom had been dogged by rumours of poor health. Health would not stop Zambians investing hopes or votes in a leader who was not too enfeebled to carry out his or her duties.

As acting president, Scott appeared to have other concerns on various issues naturally. He told The Telegraph that he was ever so worried about his personal security and that of his wife, Charlotte, in Zambia. He seemed to betray a level of mistrust for Zambia's security service as he unwittingly revealed in the newspaper interview. 'It's always going to be high-risk (being acting president),' he told The Telegraph. 'You are never quite sure to what extent they are going to try to do a Romania on you and take control of the country or if 'they' are going to just fall in.'

Scott liked making reference to 'they' for some reason despite looking out for Zambian interest as he earlier proclaimed. 'For a while, my bodyguards had rockets set up at my house,' he continued with his security concerns and some regrets about missing dinners. 'Your private life goes out the window. I can't go out for dinner anymore.'

He seemed to complain about the trappings of the office of acting president, which Edgar Lungu and other cabinet ministers seemed to have executed several times under different circumstances without a fuss.

The newspaper was quick to observe how Scott, despite his fears for his security and that of his wife, was enjoying the extras that came with the job. The 'boys' toys' that come with high office anywhere, in his case, a helicopter, and two motorcades, wrote The Telegraph. Guy said 'helping' to run Zambia brought a 'sheer sense of achievement' to him, not easily attainable elsewhere. He likened the job to a sport. 'I would have climbed the north face of the Eiger, but I'm not fit enough and I'm scared of heights, and I hate the cold,' he said, perhaps in jest.

The Eiger is a 3,970 metre mountain of the Bernese Alps, overlooking Grindelwald and Lauterbrunnen in the Bernese Oberland in Europe. Scott just used it just as an expression to show how 'on top of the world' he felt to be as acting president after getting the instruments of power from Edgar Chagwa Lungu.

In a nutshell, that was Guy Scott's crowning glory; the man who would referee the ninety day period ahead of the Zambian polls. In the eyes of Lungu's supporters, he was just the man trying his best to hamstring their man from winning the most important election in his life. He was definitely not a man after Lungu's heart.

President Edgar Lungu and First Lady Esther Nyawa Lungu on a guided tour of the Vatican following an invitation by the Holy Father Pope Francis in February 2016.

President Edgar Lungu flanked by author and diplomat Anthony Mukwita in bow-tie along Bombardier vice President Shezad Muhammed and Bombardier Africa Consortium Director Christian Bengtsson at State House meeting in April 2016.

President Edgar Lungu mingling with some diplomats accredited to Zambia in August 2016 outside the State House grounds.

Let the Bloodbath Begin

By the time President Sata was dying and Edgar Lungu was being challenged for the hottest ticket in town, the PF was no longer a small opposition party nor was Edgar Lungu a lightweight politician. The party had nationwide and international structures, a manifesto, code of conduct, and everything else that goes with an organised institution in order to help it function effectively.

Edgar Lungu was quickly becoming a household across the country, helped in large part by media coverage now concentrated on the power struggle within the ruling party. Practically, the whole country knew him or of him.

Having died just three years in office, Sata had bequeathed to Zambia a political party that was gaining in popularity, helped by a countrywide infrastructure development programme not seen since independence. Many of his supporters would have bravely ventured to propose that in Edgar Lungu, he had also left them a highly charismatic and saleable candidate, ready-made for the election due in ninety days' time.

Even with a roster of contenders long enough to field a football team, there should have been little of the mess and acrimony that ensued in deciding a candidate. Democracy, though, demanded that each candidate be given a fair shot at the opportunity to succeed the late Sata.

The rule book was pulled out and precedents consulted. There were two legally accepted ways of choosing a leader in the PF: through a party convention or through a vote passed by the all-powerful fifty-two members of the central committee.

In the eleven years since the party's formation and the contested elections, records showed that the party had gone to the convention only once. The rest of the times, Michael Sata, the only one to have represented the party in presidential elections, was elected to stand following a vote from the central committee, the supreme council of the party. Given the precedence, forty-two members of the central committee signed a petition endorsing Lungu as the sole candidate for the 20 January 2015 polls.

Guy Scott rejected this proposal, as he would with many other proposals that appeared to remotely favour Edgar Lungu. In fact, he went a step further and cancelled all meetings of the central committee and cabinet meetings, saying he wanted peace and order ahead of the polls. He wanted none of the distractions that would naturally ensue if a full-on campaign was allowed to begin even while the party's dearly departed leader's body was still lying in state.

Scott insisted political activities would only resume after his 'friend' had been laid to rest. Everyone in the ruling party seemed to see this as a genuine common sense call. The events that followed, though, would expose Scott's real motive behind his action. Scott's guise would be undone by Lungu's rising popularity among the rank and file of the PF. It was getting increasingly clear that Lungu was the party's preferred candidate, but for no good reason, it seemed that Scott's patience was beginning to wear under pressure from within.

On 3 November 2014, Scott, perhaps incapable of concealing his growing contempt for Lungu anymore, announced he had fired Edgar Lungu from his post as the party's secretary general or party chief executive officer. The announcement deliberately came in the evening, designed, it would seem, to catch Lungu and his sympathisers off-guard or incapable of mounting any sort of revolt that could not be contained under the dark of the night. Pure Gestapo.

In a press statement aired on the state broadcaster, Zambia National Broadcasting Corporation (ZNBC), Scott laid it all out—Lungu sacked. No reasons were advanced.

Lungu was at home with his wife, Esther, preparing to join the many Sata supporters that had gathered for a special thanksgiving mass in memory of the departed president at St Ignatius Catholic Church in Lusaka. This was supposed to be a special day for all friends of Sata, including Scott; a day to honour the memory of the party's founding father. So the timing did not only suck, it was totally wrong, provocative, and inflammatory. It had the potential of lighting up the country in an anti-Scott/pro-Lungu protests, and that is exactly what happened.

Edgar Lungu had already been informed of Scott's decision long before he started preparing for the event at St Ignatius, but he made no effort to address the situation, choosing instead to proceed to the cathedral. But even as he readied himself for what was sure to be a somber and emotional event, tempers were rising among sections of the party's supporters. The youth ranks were especially infuriated by Scott's decision and timing. They began baying for Scott's blood.

Led by vociferous Chief Government Spokesman, the militant, Chishimba Kambwili, the youths asked Lungu to boycott the church service and lead a demonstration against his sacking. Lungu refused. Instead, Lungu took his time, choosing an immaculate dark mourning suit to reflect the solemn occasion, and accompanied by his wife, headed for the special mass that was to be conducted by Parish Priest, Fr Charles Chilinda, at St Ignatius.

As he arrived at St Ignatius, the mood was tense among party faithful. There were people calling out to him to 'Forget the Church! Forget Mr Sata!' and 'Let us go and protest'. Others outside the church shouted, 'Scott has gone too far. Let us show him we, the members, cannot tolerate any more of this nonsense, this impunity, this is important, sir.'

Only Lungu knows how much he heard of the advice offered above the hubbub swirling about him as he walked into the church, but he did stop just long enough to state the words, 'This (the prayer service for Sata) is important. Paying respect to President Sata is very important. This church event is important, these prayers are very important. The rest we can discuss later.' Inside the church, the conversation around what Scott had done to Lungu was carried on in hushed tones.

Few would have been unaware that the ruling party's GS and chief executive officer had been fired by Guy Scott. And yet, here he was, praying and seemingly oblivious to the new development and the rising tensions outside the church. Among those that gathered for the church service was Finance Minister Alexander Chikwanda, better known by his initials, A. B. C.

Edgar Lungu sat with his wife, Esther, next to him throughout the whole service that went beyond the planned hour without showing any sign of anxiety, and looking completely unshaken by what had transpired or what was happening outside the church. He was the picture of calm before the storm.

Meanwhile, a mini civil war was brewing in the usually serene city of Lusaka, and was escalating to the politically active Copperbelt Province of Zambia, as Lungu's supporters and sympathisers heard of Scott's latest action. On Leopards Hill Road, just outside the Belvedere Government Lodge, were hundreds of people had gathered to mourn President Sata, irate youths blockaded the busy road, and started burning tyres on the tarmac.

Police moved in to deal with the situation, but not swiftly enough, as the irate youths in Lusaka and the Copperbelt continued to threaten the very peace Scott had vowed to protect at all costs. It looked like, yet again, Scott may have totally miscalculated the reaction to another of his actions against Lungu.

All the unrest occurred on Monday night stoked in part by rumours that state police had put together a team to arrest Defence Minister Lungu, and link him to the riots that occurred while he was in church.

Lungu was unperturbed, like a man protected by the some invisible shield. If there was going to be any arrest, he was fully ready for it, but he knew would not be taken alone because many supporters that had followed him from church and kept Virgil at his house had shouted that they would stay with him regardless of consequences.

On Tuesday, 4 November 2014, six days before Sata's burial, Scott was forced to swallow humble pie, rescinding his decision to dismiss Lungu in a bid to douse what was turning into an inferno within his party. It seemed that Scott just couldn't get anything correct in his hasty manner to monkey wrench Lungu's presidential bid.

Early the next morning, Scott announced he had rescinded his decision to fire Lungu, but clearly no love was lost between the two after this unfortunate ordeal that left charred tyres on Leopards Hill Road and smouldering debris across parts of the Copperbelt, evidence of the rising tempers stocked by the acting president's actions.

It transpired later, however, that Scott's decision to climb down on sacking Lungu had not been entirely of his own doing. It followed a heated meeting held with members of the central committee, some cabinet ministers, and representatives of some religious organisations, many of them reportedly telling the acting president to his face that he had fumbled big time.

The election was only weeks away, and an unnecessary civil war was the last thing the party needed at the moment—Scott was reportedly advised. Duly chastened and crestfallen, Scott issued a terse press statement stating simply, 'The position of secretary general will remain with Honourable Edgar Lungu.'

Zambians all round, especially the PF faithful, gave a sigh of relief, and everybody seemed to return to their business, leaving politics to politicians, for that is how Zambia has normally worked. They hate a prolonged, senseless fight when a peaceful and sensible solution can be found.

Before Lungu's reinstatement, Moses Siwali, a spokesman for the Home Affairs Ministry, had urged political groups to meet peacefully to resolve the situation. Lungu himself made a clarion call for peace and unity.

One commentator close to the Sata family said, regarding Scott's unceremonious dismal and hasty reinstatement of Lungu, that the Chawama MP 'became the president of Zambia the day Guy Scott fired him'.

The action had been seen by many as unjust, un-African, and aimed at nothing but belittling a man who had clearly won the hearts of many Zambians largely based on his humility—a big leadership quality in Zambia.

Scott was accused of 'insulting our culture' by some protesters in interviews reproduced by sections of local and international media. Throughout the saga of his dismissal and reinstatement, Lungu showed that a lot could be won in love and war without resorting to spilling blood or bringing down buildings.

It seemed that while many were urging him to march down the streets of Lusaka with fists upraised to protest his unfair dismissal, Lungu won the first and crucially important round in the march toward state house with his hands clasped on his laps in God's house. The key word was patience, a virtue Lungu had cultivated a long time ago in military training, legal practise, and perhaps the greatest school—life experience. That was before all the confusion that reigned when his name began to be mentioned in regards to the presidency.

Following Scott's first public loss, and Lungu's first public victory in his quest for the top job, it appeared clear that President Sata would be buried, as scheduled, on 11 November 2015 without further drama. The date, by a quirky coincidence, also marked Edgar Chagwa Lungu's fifty-eighth birthday. The office of the secretary to the cabinet had no knowledge of this happenstance, so they could not have deliberately set the birthday of Edgar Lungu as the burial date for President Sata.

On the day of the funeral, an African Union delegation, led by South Africa's Foreign Affairs Minister and AU Chair Nkosazana Dlamini Zuma, called for a stable electoral transition in Zambia as the continent showed its solidarity with Zambians who were burying a serving president for the second time in six years. 'Let us ensure a smooth leadership transition,' African Union Chairperson Nkosazana Dlamini-Zuma told thousands of mourners after a service at the National Heroes Stadium.

The Catholic Archbishop of Lusaka, the Reverend Telesphore Mpundu echoed the words, calling on Zambians to prepare for a free, fair, and transparent election that would be respected by the AU. It was a trying moment for Lungu who was a very conflicted person at this time. He was restless and tired, fatigued by the taxing responsibility of ensuring his mentor and friend, a man he loved and admired deeply, was given a fitting send-off.

Then came the moment to deliver his speech as the party's CEO. It was going well and everybody was hanging on to his every word, but halfway into his eulogy, his voice began to break, and his body started to shake. He was a broken man, and there was no masking his deep emotions even before such a massive crowd of mourners and international dignitaries. He cracked. Some commentators later said they thought it was the most moving funeral speech of any person within and outside public office they had seen in a while. The open unrestrained show of honest emotion from Lungu was overwhelming. Cynical political commentators said Lungu played on people's emotions and mourned himself into their hearts

Once he had regained his composure, Lungu made a clear reference, while not naming names, to the matter of a notorious local cartel, a group of Zambians that thought they had built Zambia Inc. believed they owned it and that they could destroy it. This group of individuals had, above all, shown immense hate and contempt for Lungu and his supporters, and had vowed to do everything in their power to wreck his ambitions to become president of Zambia. The cartel will perhaps be discussed in depth in another section of the book.

Lungu and his supporters, nevertheless, remained unmoved and were determined to show that people power, and not a section of the media nor sectional business interests nor, for that matter, money would sway them from getting the leader they wanted.

'The future of the Patriotic Front is assured,' Lungu said, adding, 'President Sata's party is not for sale to the highest bidder. Let me repeat that for emphasis. President Sata's Patriotic Front is not for sale to the highest bidder. It is for the poor and the marginalised.' His voice getting louder and firmer, he continued, 'We shall not allow personal interests and cartels driven by greed to take away the Patriotic Front. I, Edgar Lungu, shall not allow that.'

After that speech, many Zambians saw a totally new Lungu. A man who seemed to carry not just an impressive bark, he was snarling and getting ready to bite back in defence of what he believed in.

All of a sudden, people started asking whether this was the same humble Edgar Lungu they thought they knew or another Lungu had been born. Perhaps they had not had chance to listen to some of Lungu's less-than-subtle expressions betraying a tougher than thought underbelly made at various occasions when he had felt it necessary to sound a warning. 'I am a humble guy, but my humility should never be mistaken for weakness. If you step on my toes, I will fall on you like a tonne of bricks,' Lungu had said in one interview.

Lungu told the gathering that the party would carry on President Sata's vision beyond his grave, explaining that Sata was the glue that held the party together, and how he would endeavor to stay engaged with the people in the same way that Sata had done.

He closed his Sata eulogy with a few words directed at the grieving first family. 'We (PF) are your family, and in these difficult days, you can come to us and every true member of PF will be there for you. We will also call on you and count on your support.'

There was a moment here when everyone was gripped with emotion that had been building up for days. Even as he closed the speech with a few 'thank you', the grief in his voice was unmistakable. It was the grief of a student who had a lost a special teacher, or indeed a son that had lost a doting father.

With the funeral over, and the constitutional ninety days given for an election to replace a deceased president fast ebbing away, the heat was on for the PF to dispense with the formalities of naming a candidate, and drawing up a campaign strategy to sell their candidate.

Elsewhere in the opposition ranks, Hakainde Hichilema, sometimes referred to as the man with two difficult names, H. H. was not slowing down in the race for 'Plot 1' even as the grieving period continued. His well-heeled UPND campaign team kept pushing the extra political mile, mostly via TV and radio adverts and social media platforms, no doubt having paid billions of Kwacha to the likes of Muvi Television to running a highly questionable poll that placed H. H. miles ahead of Lungu. It appeared that H. H.'s campaign, having failed to deliver in three previous tilts at the job, might just pull it off this time round. It was systematic and resilient.

At what point Lungu finally made up his mind to contest the presidency is hard to tell, but there was a growing number of people—a highly voluble blend from different backgrounds—coalescing into a team that could easily identify itself as definitely pro-Lungu.

With little time to lose, the conversation quickly moved from the constant grouching and whining about Scott's attitude toward Lungu, and debating whether their man should 'go for it' to detailed planning and strategising on how to win the nomination. Before long, this band had morphed into an organised campaign team with various special responsibilities.

The crowded PF presidential field of resolute rivals did little to lift the mood at the Lungu campaign HQ. Both his internal and external rivals had huge war chests, something Lungu had in extremely short supply. What he lacked in financial means, though, he seemed to make up for with a great supporting cast of people from every run of life, dedicated to trudging the campaign trail for him, with or without money. These were people who loved him, people who believed in him, foot soldiers that were ready to stake everything on Lungu whether he won or lost, people who had known and been with him long before he became national political property.

In some meetings with his core team members, those that were with him when the sun rose and set, the author included. When the highs were high and the lows were low, Lungu would often rally them to make do with what they had rather than focusing on what they wish they had.

'Guys, it is an open secret that we have no money in our camp, but whatever little money we have, we must learn to share it for the cause. If we cannot trust each other with the little things, it will be hard for us to trust each other with the big things in future, and that future is just around the corner,' he said at one meeting. He would then distribute a few Kwacha here and there for logistics from his pocket, and move on to map out another strategy.

'I do not want you guys to leave this room without ideas of how we will win this election. I am counting on you and your support,' Lungu would say, and then step out to hold another meeting, or just chat with some supporters. He seemed to be getting good at this and really relishing the challenge.

All the while, Scott and his central committee were still shilly-shallying over a decision on the way forward for establishing a candidate for the PF. Everything remained hazy, up in the air and all over the map.

In more ways than one, this fight was so reminiscent of the Barak Obama versus Hilary Clinton primary in the United States in 2007 and 2008, as they slugged it out for the party's ticket to contest the presidency. The Grand Old Party or GOP, as the Republicans are also known, had already dispensed with the primaries and settled on John McCain, a war hero, as their candidate for the November 2008 election.

The Democrats, on the other hand, witnessed a bloody showdown between Hilary, a seasoned senator and former first lady as the wife of Bill Clinton, who was slugging it out with a junior senator out of Illinois, the little known Senator Barak Hussein Obama, an African-American born of a mother from Kansas, and a father from Kenya with nothing but an American dream. Neither Obama nor Hilary received enough delegates from state primaries and caucuses to achieve a majority without the so-called super delegate votes.

The race wasn't resolved until Clinton conceded defeat, as Obama ran up an unassailable lead in delegates, helped over the line by super delegates' pledged votes two months before the convention. In similar fashion, although the PF's super delegates (members of the central committee and cabinet colleagues) had voted for Lungu as the party's sole candidate, Scott, in his wisdom, insisted there would be no shortcuts to the presidency; and after a meeting of the central committee announced on 24 November 2014 that the party's candidate in the 20 January 2015 would be elected at a convention in the mining town of Kabwe.

It seemed Guy Scott was determined to make sure Lungu was slowed down and frustrated at every turn in his quest for the nomination. 'There will be no shortcuts in picking Michael Sata's successor,' Scott said, citing Article 58(k) of the PF constitution as the reason for the extraordinary conference to be held despite Lungu having already been overwhelmingly endorsed by the central committee and cabinet.

To outsiders and ardent political students, it appeared like a sheer waste of money and time to go for an expensive national convention, given the open support Lungu already enjoyed within the party (apart from the Scott camp) and the limited time the ruling party had to campaign while Hichilema continued to gain momentum.

In the meantime, the opposition was having a laugh and carrying half the country on their backs as the ruling party struggled to find its groove. Watching the nail-biting and infighting in the PF was, to political students, like watching a repeat of the infighting across the seas in Australia. In the fascinating election of 2013, the ruling Labour Party, under the first female Prime Minister Julia Gillard, engaged in a nasty internal fight that led to her losing to Kevin Rudd, a former prime minister.

Rudd had himself been previously ousted in a similar coup at the hands of Julia Gillard. This internal conflict set the stage for a Tony Abbot victory. Abbot was described by many students of Australian politics as a lame duck Liberal candidate who could not win a race against any credible candidate because he stood for everything the majority Australians loathed, such as gay marriages, etcetera. But he still won because the voters became tired of watching the ruling Labour party crack at the seams in a senseless internal power conflict.

Was this going to be the case in Zambia? Would the opposition candidate win because the ruling PF, under Scott as caretaker, was expending precious time and resources on a pointless internal squabble because for whatever reason, he did not want Lungu, a clear front runner, to be the man on the party ticket?

The country's scribes were watching the political red tape unfold, sharpening their pencils and scribbling furiously.

Scheduled for Saturday, 30 November 2014, the convention would leave the party and the eventual candidate with just about a month to run a nationwide campaign that had now assumed the significance of a 'life and death' affair for the PF.

A week before the convention, Edgar Lungu featured on the Red Hot Breakfast Show, a popular talk back radio programme hosted by jockeys Hope and Chi on Hot FM. Followed by wide age group said to stretch between eighteen and sixty, the platform presented a perfect springboard for Lungu to appeal to the undecided voters and let them know he was the man for the job.

Lungu also used the show to allay mounting speculation, gleefully encouraged by his enemies, to the effect that he was reluctant or plain scared of going to the convention slated for The Mulungushi Rock of Authority, outside Kabwe, to face the other ten candidates.

In response to a pointed question during the radio programme that forced the Hot FM radio station phones to ring off the hook, the now toughening Lungu said, 'I am not scared of any of the candidates within the party, and I can state categorically for the record that I will thump all of them at the convention. Let them come and challenge me.'

This was despite pundit concerns that the race was now looking shaky against a seemingly rock solid opposition led by the man with two difficult names.

There were also concerns that the acrimonious and fractious period had led to heightened internal conflict; some members of the PF, mostly those who supported Lungu, being suspended by Scott.

Instead of showing reconciliation, Scott said those under suspension would not be allowed to attend the decisive convention that could well decide the party's fate. The list of candidates still looked wrong to many Zambians for a ruling party, but that was 'the beauty of democracy', as the late President Chiluba would have said.

Those suspended by Scott for their open show of support for Lungu included the influential PF national chairperson, Inonge Wina, a 'big gun' in her own right. The party's matriarch, so to speak.

Others were Minister of Information, Joseph Katema, Jean Kapata, Willie Nsanda (the late), Stephen Kampyongo, Freedom Sikazwe, Obvious Chisala, Malozo Sichone, and Benson Chali. Others still were Fabian Chiposo, Sylvester Mtonga, John Chisanga, Lazarous Bwalya Chungu, James Kapyanga, Mwenya Musenge, and Rasford Mwale.

LUNGU'S OLD AUNT HARASSED

Leadership in Africa often comes at a cost. Sometimes, the cost is life—a jail sentence if you are lucky. Take Nelson Mandela, for instance. He spent twenty-seven years—nearly a third of his life—in prison before emerging to become South Africa's first black president after the end of apartheid. There are often few, or no boundaries at all, that desperate adversaries are prepared to respect in their quest to get what they want or to stop rivals from enjoying their democratic rights and freedoms.

For all his troubles in helping to free Zambia of colonial rule in 1964, Kenneth Kaunda found himself down a dead end street when his bete noire, Frederick Chiluba, altered the constitution in order to stop him from recontesting the presidency in 1996. Why, when K. K. wouldn't go away, Chiluba simply had him locked up for a while on some convenient charges, giving the old man enough time to transmogrify into some sort of guru, complete with a long, white beard when he finally stepped out of his cell.

It may be that Chiluba was only cashing in some long outstanding IOUs, given the treatment he had often suffered at the hands of K. K. in the days when he was a feisty, pesky trade unionist consistently getting under Kaunda's skin.

Mwanawasa suffered much verbal abuse from his knockers, of whom Michael Sata was chief, but it was water off a duck's back or 'cabbage', and he did go on to make a very decent president—the best of the lot by many Zambians' reckoning.

Sata, no shrinking violet, was gassed on more than a couple of occasions (not a good thing even for a chain smoker), roughed up from radio stations as he gave live interviews, and even served his own stint in gaol—courtesy of Mwanawasa—before achieving his own presidential ambitions in 2011.

Lungu has been running his own gauntlet of a highly critical media that has called him all sorts of names, and an equally mean conglomeration of political rivals. Accusations bordering on his personal character and integrity have been particularly hard to stomach for Lungu.

'What have I done to these friends of yours (private media masthead)? Why do they insult me like this? I am a husband, I am father, I have grown-up children. They read these hurtful insults of me every day. What do these people want from me?' Lungu is reported to have agonised before some of his inner circle as the internal jousting kicked off for the nomination to decide a PF candidate to the contest the 2015 elections.

As painful as these insults are, Lungu has experienced worse—worse than going to prison. He woke up one Sunday on November 2014 to news that an old aunt of his had been picked up by state operatives in Eastern Province for interrogation.

Milia Lungu, in her early nineties and barely able to walk on her two's was picked up on 7 November 2014 by immigration officials in Nyamphande area of his village, Petauke. Confirmed media reports said that Milia was picked up by a horde of officers, as though she were some dangerous criminal. The old woman, scared out of her geriatric bones, was questioned for several hours after being detained by officers that had taken sudden interest in knowing whether she hailed from neighbouring Mozambique or Malawi, which both border Eastern Province of Zambia.

Any other day, this could have been ignored as an isolated incident, but it just so happened that on this particular Sunday, the old woman happened to be the oldest surviving relative of Edgar Chagwa Lungu, the Minister of Defence, Minister of Justice, and Secretary General of the ruling PF. The front runner in a high-stakes political game.

'I am very surprised at this totally unnecessary and unacceptable action that has gravely traumatised my aunt,' a devastated Lungu told the media later that day. 'In Zambian or African tradition, that old woman is really my mother, and I care for her dearly.' But quickly, he pulled himself together and dared his adversaries saying, 'If you want to fight me, focus on me and not on an old, innocent woman who does knows nothing about the naked political ambitions some people harbour.'

Lungu named no names, but it was clear to many that if state agents had been sent to harass an old woman who happened to be relation of his, there could be no prizes for guessing who might have nodded them in that direction. The die was cast. 'I have said before, and I am saying now that I do not want to disrespect President Sata by engaging in divisive politics before we can even lay our beloved leader to rest. This is un-African,' Lungu told the press.

It appeared the idea behind old Milia's detention was to try to find some grounds for disqualifying Lungu from contesting the presidential race. Under the parental clause of the Zambian constitution, persons whose parents were born outside Zambia cannot contest the presidency.

President Edgar Lungu shares a cup of coffee with Chinese Ambassador to Zambia Yang Youming and United States of America Ambassador to Zambia Eric Shultz during a State House function in 2016.

President Edgar Lungu welcomes the Archbishop of Canterbury his most reverend Justin Welby when he visited Zambia in 2016 and paid his respect onto the Zambian leader.

'The man of many hats' President Edgar Lungu takes time to answer questions from the media at Kenneth Kaunda International Airport during the campaign trail in 2015. President Lungu's soft spot for hats is well known in Zambia. Mostly he dons them during weekend assignments.

THE ROCK

29 November 2014 was a huge day for Zambian politics, just eighteen days after the burial of President Sata on 11 November 2014. It started as a slow Saturday, exactly a month and twenty days before Zambians would go to the polls to elect the next president of the Southern African country.

That was the day that estranged acting president, Guy Scott, and his group of anti-Lungu supporters, the so-called Cartel, had set the day the ruling PF National Conference would take place. The party conference was intended to bring an end, once and for all, the sizzling power dispute within the PF with the party's honchos beginning to feel that quite apart from its potential to destroy the party, the infighting was becoming an embarrassment both locally and internationally.

The country's democracy, for years considered a model in Africa, was on trial, as were its fifty odd years of peace and remarkable political stability. As for Edgar Lungu, the lawyer turned politician, he was about to face the biggest personal trial of his political life.

Two days before the national conference, Lungu accepted an invitation to be a guest on a Muvi TV presidential interview. Here, he was asked to explain, perhaps for umpteenth time, what he would do as president of Zambia. Lungu articulated how he would carry on the party's vision as enshrined in its constitution, and in the words of the party's now departed founder, President Michael Chilufya Sata.

In undeveloped countries like Zambia, promises of infrastructure development are a huge part of any presidential campaign, and the candidate must be able to convince the electorate of his ability to make good his word. And so, it was that Lungu found himself explaining in interview after interview, the importance of continuing with the construction of the more than 8000 kilometres of roads countrywide, as well as the 2000 kilometres 'Pave Lusaka' roads project and many more. Lungu also needed to explain the ambitious and no less expensive plan to build some ten universities across the ten provinces of Zambia. He had to make an especially convincing case for how he intended to take development to the far-flung rural districts where poverty seems deeply entrenched.

It seemed that however hard he tried to project his vision, the opposition was unrelenting, both from within his own party, as well as from outside. He was having it rough. Figuratively, he was in the hottest part of hell. Practically, he might have felt not too far from it.

Both camps were doing their best to demonstrate that Lungu, a respected lawyer and someone who had functioned as Minister of Defence, Minister of Justice, and PF Secretary General, including acting as party president, was a clueless individual and unfit to lead the country and the party.

Lungu's opponents were spurred on by a hateful section of the private media. The Post newspaper, specifically, seemed to be set on his case. And there was the downright gutter online media whose de-campaigning efforts were, in turn, fuelled by a constant stream of accusations from Lungu's enemies inside the PF itself.

When a candidate for political office is shown no love by a strong influential opposition media or just media, things can turn quite ugly for them, as Donald Trump can attest to. And so it was that Edgar Chagwa Lungu's every deed, past and present, was held up to public scrutiny and even ridicule. With militaristic efficiency, the media (The Post) made sure that no stone was left unturned, and no sordid Lungu tale was left untold. For Lungu's supporters and most neutrals, it was hard not to taste the malice in the reportage.

Every negative thing in the aspiring candidate's life was put out there, often an exaggerated version of it, for all to see and debate. And then, of course, Lungu was blamed for any mishap, whether real or imaginary, that occurred during his time in public service. You imagined that if somebody had slipped on the proverbial banana peel and broken a leg, Lungu would have copped a fair share of the blame from some of the anti-Lungu media. From the Muvi TV interview, which was recorded just days before the party convention at Mulungushi Rock of Authority—also known as The Rock—the next stop was the widely followed and privately owned opposition-inclined Radio Phoenix, which runs a popular talkback radio programme called 'Let the People Talk'.

The slant of the interviewer was the same, as if he had been born of the same mother as The Post newspaper. Over and over again, the interviewer poked Lungu with the 'vision' question, almost as if trying to bait him to produce a specific response.

The aim was simple. Make Lungu appear as if he has no vision, zero! It was a ploy whose blowback affect the plan's masterminds had not given a second thought too, judging by the ricochet effect it had.

Lungu finally had an answer, broken down in baby formula for even the most critical of his detractors to digest. 'The party has a manifesto which the late President Sata espoused as a vision. That vision has been translated into a budget, and at this point in the race (in November), I am in no position to change that vision or manifesto. I aim to complete that which we began as a party under President Sata. If you come and ask me about my vision after 2015, I will give it to you.' Lungu's supporters were cheering, while the opposition media and his critics did their best to appear unimpressed by this common sense response.

By now, many of the PF's rank and file had been won over to Lungu, and seemed impressed by their candidate's honest explanation to many complicated and evidently biased lines of questioning by the hostile media. Like a mountain climber whose confidence soars with experience, Lungu seemed to be getting better at handling the media as the campaign progressed, and he encountered ever trickier questioning about his vision for the nation and his competence for high office.

One of his more memorable responses came on the 'Let the People Talk' show as he fenced with the interviewer and the people calling in. Scribbling notes and listening to his advisers in the booth, Lungu said, 'You cannot disband the whole army and kill all the soldiers just because the general is dead. President Sata maybe dead, but not his vision and the people that shared a vision with him.'

But why was Lungu so disliked? Among his followers and the neutrals, it was a quite a perplexing question. He was neither a murderer nor a robber nor had he made off with another man's wife. No one could prove he had committed some particularly egregious crime. He certainly had his faults, not unlike every other citizen, but there were people among his detractors who were guilty of much worse, people whose indiscretions and outright crimes had been well-documented in the media: serial adulterers, brawlers, and wife batterers.

On close investigation, it appeared most of Lungu's enemies were elitists who appeared to be intimidated by his ever-growing popularity among common folk drawn to him by his inclusive and fair style of politics that embraced everyone, regardless of their tribe, social status, or religious beliefs. Looking for faults and magnifying these through the hypercritical lenses of hostile media was his detractors' only way of trying to make Lungu look bad and unfit for high office.

By the time of the Mulungushi Rock of Authority Convention, Lungu's popularity within the PF and even outside was so high he was not only the shoo-in, he was indestructible. He was not going to give his opponents whatever their designation, shape, or size the last laugh. He had already endured all a man could endure in politics since Sata's death.

WELCOME TO THE ROCK

But just what is the Mulungushi Rock of Authority, and what does it mean to Zambia and Edgar Chagwa Lungu? Every country has a location of historic political significance. In the United States, the statue of Liberty stands as a symbol of unity and friendship between America and France and a global icon of freedom, while in South Africa, Robben Island where Nelson Mandela spent twenty-seven years as a prisoner represents that country's struggle for racial equality.

The Mulungushi Rock of Authority, situated in the Central Province on the outskirts of Kabwe Town, is probably Zambia's most important location of historic political significance. Sitting on a plot of over ten acres, the Mulungushi complex comprises university dormitories, administration blocks, and basically all the infrastructure a university needs to have.

The site is located in a rocky area near Kabwe's Mulungushi River, hence, its name. It was at first called the 'Mulungushi Rock of Ages', but later became known, perhaps as a result of the major decisions made by the UNIP Government there, as the Mulungushi Rock of Authority.

For decades, it has been a fixture in the calendars of the major political parties as the venue for their most important national party conventions. It is at The Rock that many of Zambia's major party decisions have been made, which have, in turn, made or changed the course of the nation's political history. A principal example is that of the selection of party presidents.

Just to give a flavour of some of the different parties' historical events, it was here where in 1960 the first UNIP party convention was held with Dr Kenneth Kaunda as its president. This was shortly after he and his colleagues had broken away from the Zambia African National Congress

(ZANC) Party to form the brand new UNIP, the party that was to rule Zambia from 1964 to 1991 for nearly three decades, making significant governing decisions that affected the lives of all Zambians.

To date, the Mulungushi Rock of Authority has continued to be a place where decisions are made, decisions that have had a major bearing on successive governing parties, namely the MMD and Patriotic Front. It was at Mulungushi that the PF held its first national congress after the death of Michael Sata, during which Edgar Lungu was elected the PF presidential nominee for the January 2015 elections.

Besides the selection of party presidents, making or breaking of political careers in the process, other events of national political significance have taken place at The Rock. It was here that the famous Mulungushi Reforms (or Mulungushi Declaration) of 1968 were announced through which then President Kenneth Kaunda initiated the nationalisation (Zambianisation) of a number of key foreign-owned companies including the copper mines.

To make commercial use of Mulungushi when it wasn't hosting a party's national conference, the UNIP government in 1972 established the President's Citizenship College (PCC), an institution for labour studies. Initially, its mission was to provide leadership training to officers in government, parastatal organisations, and the labour movement. Over the years, however, the college evolved into a more comprehensive training institution, first with its transformation in 1994 to the National College of Management and Development Studies (NCMDS); and then in 2007, to the fully-fledged Mulungushi University.

Twenty-ninth of November 2014, the date set for the beginning of the two-day PF party convention was a Saturday. By Friday, the twenty-eighth, hundreds of PF delegates, the ordinary party members, the foot soldiers who would be voting for their party's presidential candidate from among the many who had thrown their hats in the ring, had already been bussed into the small town of Kabwe which was now bustling with activity.

They threatened to overwhelm all its services as every bed in the lodges dotted around town was taken, and beer and water supplies quickly ran out. The feisty delegates, many of them brought in from far-out districts, had started to lubricate themselves in readiness for the conference. The normally serene Rock was alive with singing, carousing delegates. Many had already made up their minds who they wanted for president.

On Friday, 28 November 2014, Edgar Lungu had told the popular 'Let the People Talk' radio programme that he was not going to Mulungushi to lose. 'I am going to Mulungushi to win because the majority of my colleagues have already shown open confidence in me.' Lungu then proceeded to declare how he was going to 'trounce any challenger during a free and fair poll, and those that tried to throw rubbish propaganda around shall be proven wrong once and for all'. The stage for the high-stakes game was set with some 6,000 delegates in attendance, having come from all of Zambia's ten provinces.

In spite of what appeared like wild partying and carousing, the delegates were peaceful. Even they understood the ramifications that any riotous behaviour on their part would have. They could not take the chance of the election result being nullified on account of lawlessness. In addition, heavily armed riot police had surrounded the perimeter and were placed at strategic points within the premises, ready to nip any problem in the bud. Upon entering The Rock premises, all vehicles were rigorously searched, and individuals patted down to ensure that nothing at all that could be used as a weapon was allowed in.

The delegates behaved themselves even with the shortage of reticulated water at The Rock. Temporary water bowsers had been brought in, and portable toilets set up. Villagers from nearby farms and villages watched the somewhat controlled disruption to their peace with wonder. They had never seen anything like this in a long time.

Edgar Lungu arrived in Kabwe on the Friday evening of 28 November, ahead of the conference due to start the next day. He was in high spirits. He met briefly with his team, and then took an early night, so as to be well-rested the following day. It was sure to be a busy and history-shaping day for him.

On Saturday, the delegates gathered in the university administration assembly hall to elect a leader. Edgar Lungu was the sole contender for the presidency in the building. The other ten who had registered themselves as challengers for the same were conspicuous by their absence, despite their insistence on a convention, named the venue and registered the delegates on instructions from Guy Scott.

Around 10.00 a.m. the following day, Sylvia Masebo, who had recently been fired by Sata as tourism minister but was now PF Chair of Elections, majestically drove into The Rock premises accompanied by more than a dozen heavily-armed paramilitary police. She was led to the national chairperson, Mrs Inonge Wina, to whom she announced that she was the bearer of an important message from Guy Scott, acting head of state, as well as caretaker party president.

The message she brought was that Scott now wanted the convention to be held at another location in Kabwe town. Transport would be organised for the delegates already gathered at Mulungushi and now waiting eagerly to vote, to be bussed into town.

Mrs Wina saw the message not only as a joke, but also an insult to the gathering. In the first place, it was Guy Scott who had insisted on a costly convention, overriding the common sense and perfectly legal proposal by the central committee for it to adopt Lungu as the PF candidate. Secondly, it was Scott's team that had chosen The Rock venue and had even organised the registration of delegates by province in Lusaka. And now, he wanted the venue moved?

Mrs Wina, an exceptionally resolute woman working in agreement with a large part of the central committee—Edgar Lungu himself included— as well as other senior delegates, decided this new instruction was one they were prepared to ignore whatever the consequences. They smelled something fishy and decided the conference would carry on as originally planned. Here at The Rock, with or without Scott's blessing.

Masebo went back to Kabwe with her gun-totting police escort without any good news for Scott. Voting by acclamation took place in the morning, following a thorough verification of a lengthy delegates' list. The administration hall was packed to capacity, bursting at the seams with what looked like an entirely pro-Lungu assembly.

Mrs Wina announced that the convention would now break into a national conference. Later in afternoon, all verified delegates would vote from the main arena by casting the actual vote instead of acclamation, as earlier done in the morning in the administration building. There was no time to waste, Mrs Wina announced. The election of a new PF leader was going to proceed, with or without Scott's consent or presence. The law allowed her, as national chairperson, to conduct or supervise the PF's internal polls, and to preside over any other party affairs in the absence of the party president or, as in this case, the acting president.

Mrs Wina was dispatched to Kabwe town to inform Scott and his team regarding what the majority members were planning on doing at The Rock. She left instructions with the election committee to prepare the voter rolls and get verified delegates ready to cast their ballots.

Seconds turned into minutes, minutes into hours at The Rock, and delegates started to queue up. Edgar Lungu sat at the podium wearing one of his now famous hats and holding a royal walking stick, lips dry, and occasionally soothed by a bottle of water. He had not eaten lunch or indeed anything to write home about, but nothing could dim that distant, tired, but resolute glint in his eye. He could have been saying to himself, 'When does this end?'

The walking stick had been a gift from His Majesty the Litunga, King Lubosi III of the Lozi people of Western Province as a token of their friendship. The Lozi King rarely made friends with politicians nor was he well-known for dispensing gifts willy-nilly to them, so the relationship with Lungu was a rather special one.

Stories were already building up regarding the Litunga's gift to Edgar Lungu was this walking stick some kind of sceptre of authority, bestowed upon Lungu by none other than the man representing Zambia's own hundred-year-old claim to royalty?

While the preparations for the voting were going on, a steady stream of delegates were making their way to Lungu and whispering into his ear, many, it would later be known, suggesting that he seize the moment and simply declare himself the PF president since the other ten contestants had chickened out.

It could be done, but what was to be gained from such action having come this far doing the right things? He would wait until Mrs Wina returned from her meeting with Scott before deciding on his next course of action no matter how long it took. Lungu was determined to bring the presidential impasse to an end in a constitutional manner. 'We have come this far,' said Lungu. 'We might as well see the whole event through constitutionally. These good people you are seeing here have travelled from far-flung parts of the country to make a decision. We must allow them to make that decision no matter what in a constitutional manner.'

At about 15.00 hours, a visibly tired Mrs Wina returned from an extended meeting with the acting president, Scott, from Kabwe town.

Many at Mulungushi were anticipating news that Guy Scott and the ten other presidential aspirants would attend the ongoing party convention after all and face Lungu in an election.

Nothing of the sort happened. Mrs Wina reported, 'Mr Scott has refused to bring the other delegates here. Therefore, by the powers vested in me as the national chairperson, I declare the voting open. The delegates must now line up for this crucial exercise so that we can elect a leader for this great party.'

Inonge Wina was proving to be a national chairperson with teeth, and was displaying courageous leadership in a situation where the outcome of her actions could easily have gone the other way and cost her very dearly indeed. It was clear she had impressed both high and low-ranking members of the PF with her political astuteness. However, her 'iron lady' tendencies should not have surprised anyone. Inonge came from a rich political tradition being the widow of first-generation freedom fighter and politician, Arthur Wina, himself being the older of the distinguished 'Wina Brothers', renowned in Zambian politics for doing the unthinkable in those days—defying the almighty Kenneth Kaunda in the late 1980s to initiate the process that would bring multiparty politics back to Zambia. The younger Wina, Sikota, was well-known for his political astuteness and quiet demeanour that enabled him to enjoy a long political life. Sikota was also lionised for his skills as a writer.

'Let the voting begin,' announced Mrs Wina. The ballot papers, with all the eleven candidates' names listed, were distributed to the lined-up voting delegates. The whole exercise was conducted with surprising speed, and in no time, the voting was over.

On Sunday, 30 November 2014, after weeks of some of the worst political divisions ever seen in Zambia, an announcement was made by Mrs Wina. Edgar Lungu was the new president of the ruling PF, with just a little over three months to go before the national elections set for 20 January 2015.

The delegates, who the previous day had to be restrained from reacting to the provocation by Sylvia Masebo, erupted in unrestrained thunderous joy, while Lungu, hoisted high above the shoulders of jubilant supporters in images carried live across the nation via ZNBC Television, wagged his royal sceptre high in the air with a tired but triumphant arm and a radiant, toothy smile. As exhausted and relieved as he was for now, neither he nor any of his expanding band of supporters in and outside the PF would have been under any illusions about the challenges still to be hurdled on the way to the way to the big prize.

Their job done, the delegates started streaming out of the convention centre immediately after the announcement, the peaceful manner of such a boisterous procession yet again quite atypical of your regular Zambian party cadre in such instances.

As news of Lungu's election hit Kabwe, hundreds of residents made their way to line up in long queues along the road leading into town from Mulungushi, hoping to catch a glimpse of the new PF president. Many, no doubt, convinced they were seeing Zambia's new president, as his seemingly unending noisy motorcade roared into town en route to Lusaka. Kabwe Town had always had this privilege, from Kaunda through to FJT and now Edgar Lungu.

It appeared briefly that the political madness was over, and those PF members, as well as other well-wishers of the party in the country, could now sleep better. It appeared, however, that God was not yet through testing Edgar Lungu.

Guy Scott continued to show open contempt for the newly and popularly elected PF president even at the risk of fuelling violence among the different factions within the party. Scott was proving to be rather hard-headed.

Between 18.00 and 19:00 hours that Sunday, those of Lungu's supporters, who had managed to wriggle free of the snarled up traffic across Kabwe and make it in front of a TV for the main evening news on ZNBC, would have been left both deflated and frustrated. Lungu was among those who had arrived in Lusaka in time to watch the 19.00 hours main news on the state broadcaster ZNBC-TV.

The network was reporting two pieces of conflicting news, both originating from the same town and both featuring similar players—the members of the ruling party.

News item number one was what they were all familiar with 'Edgar Lungu has won the PF presidential election at party level, officially taking over from President Sata'. Good news!

In the other piece of news, Guy Scott was describing as an illegal assembly the convention at The Rock, which had seen Edgar Lungu elected as PF president. Scott was reported as having nullified the convention at the The Rock and voided the outcome of its deliberations, including Lungu's election, charging that 'the whole process was procedurally wrong, procedure was not followed, I did not participate'. Further, Scott claimed that the more than 4,000 or so registered delegates who had voted for Lungu at the party convention were ineligible, and therefore could not have been legitimately elected Lungu as PF president.

Like many a desperate man, Scott realised a little too late that he had committed a serious miscalculation by his manoeuvres with regard to the Mulungushi Convention. His response was to go on the rampage, making all manner of wild claims pulling at every straw imaginable and flexing his fast shrinking vice presidential muscle.

First, he asserted that to be legitimate, the party general conference could only have been officially opened only by him as acting president of the party. He had apparently forgotten that a clause in the party constitution, which he had helped to write, gave similar powers to the national chairperson, Mrs Wina, in this case.

Next, Scott said accreditation for his side-show—the other PF convention at the aforementioned alternate venue would go ahead. It was to take place on the next day, Monday, under his supervision and that of Masebo, still licking her wounds from being sacked by Sata.

The nation was more than mildly amused by the vacillations of the PF. The three-ring circus that had started shortly after Sata's burial had apparently not ended with the Mulungushi Rock Convention. The local TV and radio stations had never before been so closely watched or followed, as people waited in suspense for the next episode in 'PF News'.

Who was one to believe that the same ZNBC that had given live coverage of the Mulungushi Convention proceedings, which culminated in Lungu's election, or the statement from the increasingly erratic acting president? It was the worst possible time to be Richard Mwanza, the quiet director general of ZNBC who was being shot at from all angles. The different factions fighting each other within the ruling PF, plus the myriad opposition parties, all vying for air time.

ZNBC was caught between a rock and a hard place, reigniting yet again the discomfort of public-owned media during election time. Whether past experience in similar roles had made things any easier for the staff, or whether the public-owned broadcaster was having as much a field day as all other media, was not easy to say. It must, no doubt, have been quite a tightrope for ZNBC to navigate, not knowing exactly who would own you tomorrow, and thus have your future livelihood in their hands.

Scott told journalists from Kabwe on the evening of 30 November that he wanted the election of the party president to be done properly in line with the PF Constitution. Therefore, all candidates, including Mr Lungu who had just been declared winner of the PF presidency at Mulungushi, were free to contest at 'his' convention due to take place on Monday.

The other ten contestants, including GBM and Miles Sampa, both of whom were some sort of politicians to reckon with—in their own right then—had already fallen into formation. Even if he were counting the weekend's 'unopposed' win as constitutionally valid, it appeared to be a bloody awkward time to be Edgar Lungu, more so for the PF supporters in his camp—many of whom were relying on him for national direction and even personal survival in the future.

An apparently excited Masebo, as the PF elections chairperson, jumped into the fray, describing with great relish that the general conference at which Edgar Lungu had been declared PF president as 'illegal'. Everyone knew that Sylvia and Lungu were not particularly friendly toward each other. However, her publicly siding with Lungu's opponents at this particular occasion probably sealed her fate politically, as far as the PF was concerned.

The conference of the Patriotic Front chaired by Mrs Wina, however, maintained that Edgar Lungu was party president no matter what Scott and Masebo felt or threatened to do. Unfortunately for the other side, the Lungu camp had the party's constitution to back them up, not to mention the very enthusiastic court of public opinion.

President Edgar Lungu dances to a campaign song with his wife, the First Lady Esther Nyawa Lungu ahead of the 2016 crucial polls.

Edgar Lungu is welcomed by a high powered welcome party in Saudi Arabia in May 2016 when he was a guest of His Majesty the King Sulman Abdullaziz Al Saud.

Special Advisor for Political Affairs Kaizar Zulu in blue suit and Aide de Camp Chisanga 'mozegeta' Chanda flank President Edgar Lungu as he arrives at an official function.

Article 52 Sub Section 7 of the PF Constitution stipulates that a candidate, whose candidature for the office of the president of the party is approved by the national council, shall lodge his nomination papers with the returning officer appointed by the electoral commission, provided he is supported by twenty delegates from each of the provinces of Zambia.

As to the party's internal process, if more than one candidate stands for the office of president of the party, each delegate to the general conference shall vote for one candidate only, and the candidate who receives the highest number of votes shall be the sole candidate to the office of president of the republic.

The PF constitution further states that where only one candidate had filed nomination papers at the close of nomination (during the party's congress), such a candidate shall be declared the duly elected president of the party without conducting a poll. Pretty much what had happened at the Mulungushi Rock that weekend beginning Saturday 28 November 2014.

It was in consideration of this stipulation that the returning officer of the PF convention, Tutwa Ngulube, a Kabwe lawyer, declared Edgar Lungu as the duly elected party president after the other faction, also in Kabwe at the time, failed to show up at the original convention venue.

Mrs Wina, scoffing at the threats from the 'other camp', bravely reaffirmed that Edgar Lungu had been duly elected as PF president and was, consequently, the presidential candidate of the ruling party in the forthcoming national race of 20 January.

For her part, Mrs Wina had done her best in her capacity, as national chairperson of the PF, to persuade the other camp to attend the conference as was originally planned. In snubbing his party's national chairperson, Scott, even at the cost of injured pride, had overlooked an immense opportunity to work for the party's unity and also prepare to fight a common enemy—other opposition parties. At this time, it would have been clear to the neutral observer that whatever his agenda, Scott had carried it inexorably and irreparably too far. Much more.

Meanwhile, preparations for a second convention continued in Kabwe, which was scheduled to start Monday, first of December. Lungu's aides gathered at his home for urgent strategising sessions on Sunday evening. It was decided that waiting for Monday to act when Scott had shown open defiance to The Rock poll would be leaving a crucial decision too long. A decision and action had to be on Sunday night.

Edgar Lungu, as resolute as ever, was not about to leave anything to chance. By the time the nullification was being announced, Lungu had officially filed, in his presidential interest, papers or nomination papers before the Electoral Commission of Zambia.

By filing in his presidential interest papers, Lungu had effectively given up his position as party secretary general. He received his nomination papers as PF's candidate for the national presidency at a sold-out event held at a sports club located between the Arcades Shopping Mall and the Lusaka Show Grounds. As the presidential campaigning got underway, Lungu successfully fended off attempts by the Scott group to strip him of the positions of Minister of Defence, Minister of Justice, and Chair of the PF Party Disciplinary Committee. This resistance, of course, happened before and after The Rock.

It appeared that the rationale behind divesting Lungu of his many titles, his many hats, was to try to limit the considerable influence he wielded through his many offices to influence the outcome of the polls; and yet, there was nowhere in the constitution where a candidate was required to lay aside any of his party or government titles to qualify for nomination as the party's presidential candidate. However, Lungu's detractors were stopping at nothing in their quest to deny him any advantage.

Scott had already ensured that Lungu enjoyed no incumbency privileges such as the unfettered use of the presidential private jet, The Challenger, for his cross-country campaign trips. Lungu had to pay for everything, just like an opposition candidate would.

Scott's open contempt for Lungu was almost like that of a proud master writing off an ordinary person in the village. It was almost like the doomed-to-execution medieval King Charles telling the Lord protector, Oliver Cromwell, in the 'English History of Democratisation' that 'you cannot expect extraordinary deeds from ordinary people, cobblers, and basket weavers'. In this case, Edgar Lungu being the basket weaver, and Scott the King or gentry.

EXPLAINING THE GBM FACTOR

The relationship between Edgar Chagwa Lungu and Geoffrey Bwalya Mwamba, also known as GBM, was not always acrimonious as it turned out after Michael Sata's death—at least not at the face of it.

Both men were close to President Sata, albeit for different reasons. Lungu offering legal services at a time many lawyers would be too busy to take up the sort of protracted and often politically incorrect, not to mention unprofitable legal problems Sata often attracted.

GBM (Great Bag of Money, as some like to jokingly refer to him. He also had a rather unflattering moniker of GBV. This was attributable to his spectacular recorded history of violence that is well documented in Zambian media) on the other hand, offered, as he often openly bragged, the much-needed financial muscle in addition to the money stream that was already flowing steadily into the Sata opposition political machinery from other sources. There is certainly no public evidence that GBM and Lungu never got on. In fact, the first time Edgar Lungu was called to act as president by Sata in 2012, he had been on an international tour of duty with GBM in the Democratic Republic of Congo (DRC).

President Sata had sent both ministers to go and attend a joint security meeting as Minister of Defence and Minister of Home Affairs, respectively, but Lungu was asked to cut his trip short for the first time to return home to serve as acting president—the first of at least three times this would happen before Lungu became president.

It appeared that the fallout happened during the power struggle that ignited within the PF after Sata's passing. GBM was among the group of PF heavyweights that contested the eventually discredited, Scott-arranged convention in Kabwe, and was shunned by the parallel convention presided over by PF national chair, Inonge Wina, that elected Lungu as the party's candidate in the 2015 presidential poll.

On 1 December 2014 at Government House, Scott led a fragile 'peace coalition' where all the PF members that had failed in their quest to win the right to replace Sata came together to pledge their support to Lungu as the preferred party ticket candidate, GBM included.

After the kiss and makeup, the likes of Chishimba Kambwili, Given Lubinda, and Wylbur Simuusa, all Members of Parliament, quickly rallied behind Lungu, accompanying him on provincial tours, and even endorsing him openly in television adverts but not GBM. He kept his distance.

Insiders say some of Lungu's inner circle then began to receive messages meant for the presidential candidate, asking him to initiate discussions with GBM to talk about campaign funds. Whether the initial approach came from GBM himself is not known, but there were enough of Lungu's circle who urged him to take up the offer. It is reported that during one such conversation with the GBM emissaries, Lungu took umbrage. 'I do not need his money. In fact, I do not need any money from anyone who might hold me to ransom after the elections because of their money.'

The emissaries from GBM increased in numbers as the resources became dear and Scott tightened the tap against Lungu, but with each and every emissary, Lungu's resolve to reject the money increased. 'I do not want dirty money. I will win or lose this campaign with or without GBM's money. I will not go and kneel down for GBM for help. His money is the last thing I need on this campaign or any other for that matter,' he said on another occasion.

GBM subsequently left the PF to join the UPND, and would be joined on the opposition party's campaign tours ahead of the 2016 general elections by other former PF stalwarts like Guy Scott and Miles Sampa where they continued to denounce Lungu's reign, alleging corruption and other vices.

THE INJUNCTION

Edgar Lungu had millions of people behind him in those exhausting, uncertain days who were ready to work with and for him to ensure that justice, as perceived by the majority, was served. This meant seeing the whole project through to Lungu being installed as national president, the president of Zambia, just as he seemed to have been anointed to be.

Among the millions now working for and with Lungu was a team of five—three lawyers and two journalists. So, enter Kelvin Bwalya Fube (KBF), Emmanuel Mwamba, Sukwana Lukangaba, Anthony Mukwita (the author), and Bokani Soko—in all a considerably formidable combination.

A meeting had been convened at Edgar Lungu's residence off Brentwood Drive upon the group's return from the convention. There were urgent matters on the table: the news that Scott would continue with his own convention, even hold an election to be chaired by Masebo on Monday. In attendance were a significant number of PF members including the other candidates in contention for the party's presidency who had failed to show up at the Mulungushi Convention.

Among those gathered at Lungu's residence that evening were a number of party stalwarts. The list included Party Secretary General Davies Chama and Samuel Mukupa who would later become Lungu's campaign manager. Given Scott's continuing machinations and pronouncements against Lungu, the meeting felt something a damp squid, the post–convention euphoria having quickly dissipated as Lungu's triumph in Kabwe was thrown into uncertainty. The gathering decided that it was not enough to keep getting mad at Scott's divisive and frustrating actions. They decided to get even and take the fight right up to Scott's doorstep.

Until his appointment as President Lungu's special assistant for legal matters, Lukangaba was a junior lawyer at Mweemba Chashi and Partners of Lusaka. KBF ran his own law firm, while Soko was in imports and exports and not practising court law. Soko was a businessman.

Mukwita and Mwamba were working full-time on the Lungu media campaign team along with others such as Bennadete Deka, Sunday Chanda, Kaizar Zulu, Emmanuel Chilubanama and Brian Hapunda.

The firm's (Mweemba Chashi and Company) office was located just behind Handyman's Paradise in Lusaka's Northmead residential area. Kelvi Bwalya Fube was leading the legal team and also organising cadres.

It was just after midnight in Lusaka. Most people had gone to bed after Kabwe in preparation for the new week starting tomorrow, but for some key Lungu strategy members, there was to be no sleeping, not this night.

Team Lungu had their orders: use the law against the Scott camp to ensure it was their convention that would be declared illegal, and their election results nullified, while Lungu's election must be upheld as legitimately convened. The team of five, tired to the bone after Kabwe, but united and strengthened by their dislike of Scott's manuervers, jumped into separate cars and drove to the Northmead office of Mweemba Chashi and Partners.

Emmanuel Mwamba, Zambia's High Commissioner to South Africa (at the writing of this book), also a former permanent secretary in the Ministry of Information, vividly recalls how, when they reached the law firm, Lukangaba had no keys to open the iron-cast gate.

'But because there was no time to waste, after hooting several times in order to get the attention of the housekeeper', Mwamba recalls, 'Anthony bravely (Mukwita) offered to scale the high wall and go inside the premises to wake up the housekeeper, whom he did not even know and who did not know him either. It was a daring thing to do, but Anthony just did it.'

The group, mere silhouettes against the light and shadows of a quiet night, watched Mukwita scale the wall, walk briskly to the caretaker's house, knock several times, and eventually come back with the caretaker to open the gate.

Here, volumes of law books were opened side by side with the PF Constitution—the party's own law book. The lawyers, working side by side with the journalists, tore apart and dissected what needed to be dissected, and analysed whatever needed to be analysed. The idea was to ensure that the planned 'sabotage' meeting plotted by the Scott-Masebo team would never see the light of day.

The job involved examining precedent, as well as anticipating every next move, statement, and action of the Scott camp. The idea was to ensure that at the end of the day, the book was thoroughly thrown at them in every possible department that they would never find a way of coming back. So the lawyers, KBF, Soko, and Lukangaba worked the textbooks, while the journalists, Mukwita and Mwamba, used their speed and analytical skill to interpret the law and present it in everyday language that ordinary people could easily relate to in order to type the court arguments for Lungu.

In addition, old legal and court contacts were revived and favours called in by the lawyers, so that by 0700 hours on Monday morning, everything needed to obtain a court order to stop what analysts have since called a sham poll were in place.

The court registry was opened up, and a judge was found to sign the injunction in the dead of night following the team's resilient work that saw them burn the midnight oil with not a wink of sleep. By eight o'clock the following morning, a helicopter was in the air carrying one of the most prized documents of the Lungu election campaign—an air-tight injunction restraining Scott and Co from disrupting the due process of the law and possibly plunging the nation into an abyss of chaos.

The five-man team then retired to their separate homes at about 8.00 a.m. from the previous night to freshen up, and maybe grab a bite before launching right back into the long unbroken day that had started Sunday morning.

Apparently, not all legal loopholes had been sealed to the letter. The parallel Kabwe poll was going ahead as scheduled. Scott and Masebo had declared it business as usual in defiance of the recently-served injunction. Unconfirmed reports say that the bearer of the 'bad news injunction' was roughed up a little before being told to get away from where the parallel elections were going on.

ZNBC had continued to broadcast the Scott-led convention and polls live, raising the collective eyebrows of the viewing public who, two days before, had also watched the Mulungushi proceedings. It was time for the Lungu camp lawyers to again take some action. The only way to knock the wind out of the Scott camp was to stop the live television broadcast, and for that to happen, they would need to read the riot act to ZNBC. Richard Mwanza, the hapless ZNBC director general, was shown the injunction that had been obtained from the court earlier that morning, and informed that by continuing to broadcast the proceedings at the other convention, he and the institution he ran were in breach of several statutes.

Everyone who knows Mwanza knows that he is not only a gentleman, but a God-fearing man and law-abiding citizen. He read the injunction and pulled the plug off the Scott poll saying he did not want to contribute to the likely blowout between the two PF factions nor indeed to risk the jobs of any ZNBC employees, including his own. He decided to respect the injunction so far as it affected ZNBC.

As the first heavy cloud of darkness descended upon the Scott election, which was no longer to be legitimised by ZNBC commentary, things began to look rather shaky for Scott and his supporters. By the end of the day, Scott had lost another round to Lungu. With the clock ticking toward the national poll, the party's central committee issued a nomination certificate, making Edgar Lungu the only bona fide elected president of the ruling PF, the second one after the death of President Sata. A press conference was organised to be held at the Mulungushi International Conference Centre in Lusaka (MICC), which was to be aired live by ZNBC and others such as Hot FM radio. Once again, the nation was on a cliffhanger, not knowing what was to come of this event in the ongoing media circus.

Lungu's foes had probably anticipated a big event, but they were completely unprepared for what actually happened. The brother from Chimwemwe and Chawama who, many had once dismissed as a political upstart going nowhere very fast, drove into Mulungushi International Conference Centre. With him came the most overwhelming mass of supporters seen around a candidate for political office in Zambia in recent times. The air was filled with such Lungu mania that even toddlers were saying his name—Edigar!

However, as much as this day seemed to be a bright spot in a long period of grey, the twists and turns were not yet over. The chapter was not yet complete in one of the most intriguing tale of Zambia's political life. The show, it seemed, was still going on. During the Mulungushi International Conference Centre event, Lungu had the important job of proving to any doubting Thomases still around that in case they didn't know, the new boss was in town, and his name was Edgar Chagwa Lungu.

Edgar proceeded to strike the first blow. First to be axed was Sylvia Masebo who had presided over the now shamed parallel elections held in Kabwe on Monday, the first of December 2014. Her political career was over for the foreseeable future. The axe, also after Lungu's rock election along with her co-conspirators, Anthony Kasolo and Bridgette Attanga. It was over for them just like that.

Guy Scott, to the dismay of the rank and file, survived. Did this make him friendlier to the Lungu cause? Not at all, but he continued to cause harm to Lungu's candidature through various underhanded methods and plain dirty politics. Still, Lungu was merely biding his time just waiting for the right moment.

When the rank and file insisted that Scott should also face the axe, Lungu yet again shocked all. 'I am not in a hurry to punish people, neither did I vie for this position to punish real or perceived enemies. I am here to unite a fragile party and a divided nation,' he would often say when asked when he would sack Scott and others who had openly insulted him.

However, despite this conciliatory gesture, Lungu still faced a real and present enemy in Scott. The acting president had, from the look of things, promised himself that he would curtail Lungu's chances of becoming president of Zambia, whether by hook or by crook.

On 16 December 2014, while still acting PF vice president, Scott, wrote Acting Chief Justice Lombe Chibesakunda and warned her 'not to entertain anyone' who would identify themselves as a PF presidential candidate as long there remained court disputes in place, regarding the party leadership. Such contempt. The court dispute Scott was referring to was a matter regarding the parallel poll, the one which had been written off as a sham by the Scott team's own returning officer.

The Scott team had initially engaged Germano Mutale Kaulungombe, a Lusaka lawyer, to front their sham poll, but he refused to sell out his buddies in the PF. As a backup, Kaulungombe abided by a court order, which prohibited him from declaring anyone a winner in the Scott-Masebo poll.

Kaulungombe said the poll he had initially agreed to preside over had failed to meet the minimum standards set by the Electoral Commission of

Zambia (ECZ) or any other electoral body for that matter. Also, as a court officer of high repute, Kaulungombe said he did not want his name linked to disobeying court orders. Not even Scott saw this one coming, it seems.

By now, people were wondering aloud why Scott was so determined to openly stop a party colleague from running for president. Why he was so hell-bent on frustrating the one candidate that PF had, who was strong enough to beat contenders from the other political parties and had widely been accepted by the party rank and file? Why was he working against the person most likely to retain his party in government, and this so close to election date, less than one month or thirty days when there likely would not be any time to repair any damage to the PF? For instance, Scott de-campaigning Lungu, as he was doing, was effectively campaigning for the opposition leader, Hakainde Hichilema (HH). It was shocking but true.

The result? H. H.'s numbers continued to improve in the media polls, while the PF effectively did its best to self-destruct. The reason given by Scott in his 16 December letter to the chief justice was an explanation that had recently become his mantra—his commitment was to ensure the party followed its own procedures as outlined by the PF constitution. However, as much as he said this, he convinced few.

Lungu remained unmoved. Just as had been the case when Scott fired him on the eve of Sata's memorial mass at St Ignatius, the acting president's malicious monkey wrench seemed to have failed to work yet again. Edgar Lungu was now unstoppable. Scott had a tough choice to make at this point, either join Lungu or lose him forever.

Most of the other PF presidential aspirants who had earlier stood against Lungu had now openly reconciled with him and taken their places behind him for the sake of the party, and most importantly, for the sake of the nation. They had the good sense to realise and accept that Lungu was the party's undisputed choice. Perhaps in a moment of clarity, or perhaps a moment of magnanimity, or both, Chishimba Kambwili, in his capitulation from opposing Lungu, called him the 'man of the moment'. Kambwili was echoing the sentiments of all PF members, whether or not they were friends of Lungu.

Others, such as the veteran Kabwata lawmaker, Given Lubinda, described Lungu as a person with deep belief in humanity who knew how to embrace people from various social divides, be they rich or poor, and to make them all feel needed and equal.

In all this, Sata's widow, Dr Christine Kaseba Sata, remained loudly silent. Her initial interest in contesting the presidency to replace her husband had been loudly condemned by large section of the Zambian people as 'too soon', forcing her to silently withdraw from the race.

Edgar Lungu, who was still operating as Minister of Defense, Minister of Justice, and now also president of the ruling PF, welcomed back all those ready to reconcile. That is politics. It is also just Lungu's style, although some would, in future, question the wisdom of all this inclusiveness.

Now, totally on the campaign trail, the 'man of the moment' arrived in Lusaka after yet another thunderous rally in Ndola, the politically active mining town where he was born and where he made his final Copperbelt call.

On 19 January 2015, the eve of the election, Edgar Lungu addressed a rally at Woodlands Stadium attended by what appeared like double the crowd that his main rival H. H. had pulled at an earlier meeting at the same venue. The crowd was ecstatic, and at this point, it seemed as though he had already sealed the poll and was only a step away from becoming the sixth president of Zambia. To add to the excitement, he was joined on the stage by dozens of popular Zambian musicians such as JK, who were doing their bit to work the crowd.

Apart from the usual support cast who went everywhere Lungu went, including many who had been with him from the beginning, there were some who had joined in along the way and were with him on the podium at this last rally before the election.

Interestingly, up there, throwing his support behind Lungu, was Zambia's fourth president, Rupiah Banda. Alongside him, a rather subdued Dr Scott. Had he been won over or simply been beaten, a case of 'if you can't beat them, join them'? Indications were that it was more the latter.

Former Republican President, Rupiah Banda, was a different story though. In the usual vagaries of politics, Lungu had somehow won the support of a man who had been a bitter rival of the late Sata, and who now looked to be delivering possibly the entire Eastern Province, his home region, to the PF on a silver platter.

In opposition circles, H. H. had held his own final rally in Mandevu area after a poorly attended one on Sunday at Lusaka's Woodlands Stadium, a dripping afternoon sky doing him no favours—the same venue where Lungu was now holding his last rally. At this point, it looked like going to the polls at all was more of an academic exercise; just a matter of crossing the *T*s and dotting the *I*s. Still, Lungu would not begrudge himself one last dig at Sylvia Masebo, saying, 'There is nothing I have done to this woman (Sylvia). The same thing I have not done to her is the reason she resents me.'

Delivered in Bemba (*'Filya fine nshamu chita, efyo ampatila'*) the put-down seemed to go down really well with the crowd, touching off a wave of raucous laughter and some half-embarrassed giggles. The next day, on the evening of the polls, Scott pulled out another perplexing rabbit from his hat, giving permission to an opposition team to fly into the voting zone against electoral regulations.

The Zambia Air Force under Lt. General Chimese, nevertheless, also saw it as a breach of the electoral laws, which forbid campaigning on election day, and so denied the opposition UPND team clearance to fly against Scott's orders.

Twentieth January 2015, finally, the day everyone had been waiting for. Being the height of the rainy season, it was bucketing down in Lusaka, but scores of enthusiastic voters were determined to defy the weather, queuing up at their various polling stations from early morning under umbrellas.

The campaigns had been done. Now, the people were about to speak, and although what they would say by the end of the day could not be known for sure, there were some among the PF faithful who sensed an element of predictability in this election.

Edgar Lungu woke up early that morning, put on a black leather coat, a pair of burgundy pants, and his now famous flat cap and headed for the polling station. His destination was, without question, his constituency, Chawama, south of Lusaka. He cast his vote at Andrew Mwenya Polling Station between Chawama and John Howard Townships. True to nature, Lungu had registered to vote right there in the overcrowded, poorly serviced township where some of the poorest people of Lusaka lived. Accompanied by his wife, Esther, and the usual crowd of supporters, he was among his own. He went about casting his vote in as business-like fashion as he could to muster in the circumstances to avoid breaking any laws against campaigning on polling day and promptly left.

Lungu's main rival, and the only other credible contender for the presidency in this election, Hichilema, was scheduled to cast his vote at an undisclosed location in the upmarket Kabulonga residential area. Kabulonga is the Beverly Hills of Lusaka where some of the richest people in the country live. This dynamic is an important one to note, as in any election, the ability to connect with people of all classes is crucial and can make or break a candidate's chances.

The Lusaka downpour slowed down the voting, somewhat with records showing that the turnout that day was not one of Lusaka's most impressive in recent history. Nevertheless, enough of the population turned up countrywide to make it a credible poll.

A team of election monitors from the Southern African Development Corporation (SADC) chose to start witnessing the voting in Chawama were Lungu was voting from before proceeding to other parts of the city. By 18.00 that evening, the SADC team, led by South Africa's Foreign Affairs Minister, Madam Maite Nkoana Mashabane, pronounced the voting process as having met international standards. That meant that the team had not observed any significant evidence of misconduct in any of the election-day processes.

Having done their part, Zambians retired back to their homes to await announcement of the results. The counting had commenced immediately. The opposition had their own private voter tabulation (PVT) in place to verify all results.

The PF had done its own as well, confident it had perfected the process after many previous hits and misses during Sata's several previous failed attempts at the presidency. The Electoral Commission of Zambia (ECZ) had a tough job administering the elections with ten provinces and over seventy districts and 150 constituencies to manage. In all, there were over 1,000 polling stations across the country.

Collecting ballots from some of the far-flung areas of rural Zambia to a central constituency tallying centre is a challenging enough feat during the best of times. During the wet season, with roads in these parts rendered impassable, the exercise becomes something of a mission. Without the involvement of the Zambia Air Force, this would be mission impossible.

For its part, the ECZ did a commendable job giving blow-by-blow updates of results as they came in, hot from the tallying centres. The national tallying centre was located at MICC in Lusaka where results were announced to the media and the public constituency by constituency as they came in after verification.

After several presidential and general elections since the return to multiparty politics in 1991, Zambians know that they cannot expect a presidential poll result to be returned the same day of voting, so they cast their vote and go home to enjoy what is usually a quiet holiday, following the results, as they are announced by the ECZ via radio and television.

Early in the counting, the major provinces indicated an early lead for Lungu, ahead of Hichilema in a two-horse race. PF supporters were praying it was a harbinger of things to come.

During one of his campaign speeches, Lungu had said, 'The peoples' voice shall be the peoples' choice. I have already pledged to be a servant of the Zambian people, but ultimately, they have the final choice, and I hope it is I they will choose.'

From the PF PVT tallying, it emerged that Lungu was leading in votes counted in the Northern Province, Luapula Province, Eastern Province, the Copperbelt, and Central Province. He also had a strong showing in Western Province and North Western Province, but the ground appeared shaky for him in Southern Province, a known stronghold of rival, Hichilema.

Something strange was happening in the Southern Province that was unprecedented in Zambia's voting history. Lungu, a leading presidential candidate from the ruling party, was getting hardly any votes at all. Hichilema, his rival, was winning every vote counted. Stranger still, almost all registered voters in his area were turning up to vote. It was a quite bizarre turn of events.

President Edgar Lungu receives salutations in his honour as a guest of the President of China His Excellency Xi Jinping in Beijing in March 2015.

President Edgar Lungu exchanges pleasantries with Tanzania's President Jakaya kikwete.

President Edgar Lungu converses with the King of Swaziland, His Majesty King Mswati III in gold neck tie as the first female vice President of Zambia Mrs Inonge Wina follows the conversation. This was in 2015 when King Mswati III visited President Lungu shortly after his first election victory.

THE DECLARATION

In all, two million people had voted in the January 2015 elections out of a possible 5.4 million registered on the roll. As unfavourable as the weather conditions were, the ECZ managed to bring in, count, and tally every single vote that had been cast in the election. On the fourth day of counting and with only four constituencies remaining out of 150, the ECZ decided they had a winner. On 24 January, the announcement was made. Edgar Lungu had tallied 789,848 votes from 146 constituencies, while Hichilema came in with 776,832. The remaining constituencies: Mafinga, Chama North, Chama South, and Mfuwe, all of them PF strong-holds, made chasing after results from these areas a purely academic exercise. Hichilema had made a real fist of it, but once again, he had come a cropper.

Here for the record, are the ECZ official numbers:

Up to 5,074,937 Zambians had registered to vote in 2015, but the number that actually braved the rains to go and vote stood at 1,646,867. Total voter turnout was 32.45 per cent. There was a percentage of damaged ballots not been included in the number of those counted before the declaration. In the end, Lungu had edged Hichilema by 27,757 votes, a narrow majority of 1.66 per cent but nevertheless, a majority and victory under the 'first-past-the-post' system prevailing at the time.

While Zambians had gone home to sleep on polling day and had stopped campaigning, Hichilema, perhaps sensing defeat, decided to hire choppers to fly into some undisclosed voting areas. However, an alert air force thwarted the suspicious efforts.

A source from within the air force said the action of Hichilema's UPND was a violation of the laws governing polling, which did not allow anyone, regardless of the party they belonged to, to continue campaigning after the time, for this was officially closed. Guy Scott, though fully aware of the law, had surprisingly given permission for Hichilema's choppers to fly into selected areas at short notice after the campaign period was legally over.

The choppers never left the ground. Many shudder to think or even fathom what could have happened. If at the last minute Hichilema had been allowed to fly to those areas that dark, rainy evening.

In a public statement, Hichilema bemoaned ZAF's failure to grant flight clearance for his choppers, saying, 'ZAF continued to delay in granting us clearance with no clear reason.' Hichilema neglected to mention that electoral regulations made it illegal to campaign beyond 1800 hours on the eve of elections. Scott offered no explanation for his own decision, but that shouldn't have surprised anybody. Scott had shown himself to be a non-supporter of Edgar Lungu; he opposed him to the very last day.

After declaring Lungu the winner of the election on the night of 24 January 2015, the ECZ then set in motion the process that would see him inaugurated as the sixth president of Zambia. The swearing-in ceremony was set for the next day, 25 January 2015, at the Heroes Stadium in Lusaka. Lungu was finally where he had set out to be three long months earlier, serving the remaining period of President Sata's tenure, which was due to end in September 2016.

There was a burst of spontaneous celebrations across the country, as Lungu's supporters, church groups, and some civil society groups ululated. The election process and behaviour of the electorate were endorsed, and the elections certified 'free and fair' by local and international monitoring groups. Among the many monitors were Christian organisations domiciled in Zambia including the Christian Churches Monitoring Group (CCMG), which is made up of the influential Zambia Episcopal Conference (ZEC) and its affiliates, Catholic organisations such as Caritas and the Jesuit Centre for Theological Reflection (JCTR), as well as the Council of Churches of Zambia (CCZ). The CCMG issued a statement saying, 'Based on the findings of the CCMG's PVT, Zambians should have considerable confidence that the official results as announced by the ECZ reflect the ballots cast at polling stations.'

Congratulatory messages were received from SADC chair, Robert Mugabe, who thanked Zambians for a good election. The United Nations Secretary General, Ban Ki Moon, also sent word congratulating the Zambian people for the peaceful manner in which the country had organised the elections despite difficult weather conditions.

Edgar Lungu, who had turned fifty-eight the day Michael Sata was put to rest, was able to celebrate his birthday in style—as president of the Republic of Zambia.

Commander-in-Chief Edgar Lungu is flanked by the Zambia Airforce (ZAF) Commander aka ZAFONE Lieutenant General Eric Chimese during the annual ZAF officer's ball in Lusaka. President Lungu is accompanied by the First Lady Esther Nyawa Lungu.

'So Help Me God'

It is Sunday, 25 January 2015, and Edgar Lungu is standing tall, pensive, and attentive before the acting chief justice of the Supreme Court of Zambia, Her Ladyship Mrs Lombe Chibesakunda, before a packed National Heroes Stadium in Lusaka. He is about to utter arguably the most important words he has ever spoken in his life, bar his marriage vows.

'I, Edgar Chagwa Lungu, having been constitutionally elected to the office of the president of the Republic of Zambia, do swear that I shall perform the functions of this high office, that I will faithfully and diligently discharge my duties, that I will uphold and protect the constitution without fear or favour, so help me God,' the newly-elected president of Zambia says to wild cheers from a massive crowd packed into the stadium, the tannoy carrying the voice into the nearby townships.

Before and around him, and the crush of media and security personnel, is a heaving sea of green and white. The thousands of animated PF supporters clad in party colours who have crammed into the cavernous stadium, occupying every available space all the way to the rafters. Many have travelled hundreds of kilometres from the outer reaches of the country to witness the celebrations.

January is normally the height of the rainy season in Zambia, but on this day, the weather is great. The sun shines brightly and the winds remain calm, almost as if bidden by the gods. The usually long drive from David Lewanika close, off Brentwood Drive near state house where Edgar Chagwa Lungu resided, had been a smooth one. Not for him anymore the daily hustle of battling through the manic Lusaka traffic, the tiresome, daily lot of motorists living in one of the most densely peopled cities in the world.

Leading the presidential cavalcade as it sped to the stadium for the inauguration was a slew of security escort vehicles from the Zambia police, army, and air force. Their sirens and shimmering red, yellow, and blue lights forcing traffic to the sides, a little like the Biblical parting of the Red Sea by Moses and his rod. All along the entire route, thousands of people of all ages waved enthusiastically as the procession zipped past.

The journey had started with Edgar Chagwa Lungu easing himself into the gleaming (black) Mercedes Benz limousine parked outside his ministerial house that morning. He walked toward the car as a guard opened the door, froze to attention, and saluted him with his clasped hands resting just above his waist like a supplicant walking into his prayer closet. It was a posture that would become all too familiar to observers, a gesture of humility that would endear him to millions of Zambians as the unassuming lawyer and member of parliament from one of Lusaka's poorest constituencies stepped into the most coveted job in the land.

Instead of a registration plate, presidential limo displays a huge, gleaming copper eagle emblem. Copper and the fish eagle have a special, iconic place and meaning in Zambia. The eagle is the national bird of the country, as it is of Zimbabwe, Namibia, South Sudan, and South Africa, a symbol of power, majesty, and independence. Copper has been synonymous with Zambia since the early 1900s when the country was still under colonial rule. Over half a decade since independence, the red metal remains Zambia's premier export product and source of wealth, accounting for more than three-quarters of the country's foreign currency receipts despite repeated attempts by various administrations to diversify the economy.

Like his string of predecessors, Edgar Lungu would soon have his own experience grappling with the consequences of a mineral-dependent mono-economy as the international price bottomed out and skittish mining companies began to release thousands of workers onto the streets of the politically sensitive Copperbelt and North Western Provinces. But that is not on his mind at this moment. He would savour the hour even if it amounted to no more than a momentary respite from what had been a brutal campaign that began with a messy succession war within the PF in the aftermath of the death of founder, Michael Chilufya Sata, and the multiple and complex tasks that awaited him as a substitute-president thrust into the job with just over a year to the next election.

Decked out in a simple, but immaculately cut royal blue two-piece suit tailored to fit his slender, athletic frame, Edgar Lungu was the picture of sartorial elegance as he pronounced his oath of office. The suit hung neatly on him like a hand in a glove. It was complemented by a snow-white shirt and a trendy narrow blood-red 1960s style necktie that cut short its journey just around the belly button. A white handkerchief peeped over the top left breast pocket of the jacket.

This was Edgar Lungu's first suit as president of Zambia—the first cut; and the last one he would wear as Minister of Defence, Minister of Justice, President of the ruling Patriotic Front (PF), Member of Parliament for Chawama Constituency, and Secretary General of the PF, to mention but a few, for Edgar Lungu was man who wore many hats, both figuratively and literally.

A spry 58-year-old, Edgar Lungu could easily have passed for forty something years or even younger. Women thought he looked sexy, that he was to die for, while men wanted to be him, and have women die for them.

The adage 'It is not the suit that maketh the man, but the man that maketh the suit' was immediately thrust back into the narrative by Edgar Lungu in the blink of an eye, as his motorcade swivelled past state house on to Independence Avenue to the right of the road—his future home. The motorcade did not use the normal route, but took the one preferred by motorists heading east to Ibex Hill or Woodlands in the opposite direction where the road had been swept clean of all other vehicular traffic, allowing only the presidential motorcade and pedestrians.

The drive continued past the colonial-styled cabinet office that houses three of Edgar Lungu's former offices, the Ministries of Defence, home affairs, and justice, as well as the office of the vice president were only some three years ago, he had served as an understated junior minister.

The police headquarters, so-called force headquarters, the red-brick building with its uninviting, ominous-looking façade stood to the left of the road opposite the Foreign Affairs Ministry, or Charter House, as you drive north before reaching the roundabout.

The supreme court and high court buildings stood to the right. A little over three years ago, Edgar Lungu had been among the hundreds of thousands of people that had besieged the courts as Michael Chilufya Sata took oath of office after ousting Rupiah Banda of the MMD.

Turning left at the roundabout, the convoy swiftly slid into Church Road on past the Southern Sun Ridgeway Hotel on the left and the Anglican Cathedral on the right, past the Zambia National Service HQ and Taj Pamodzi Hotel to the right, down toward the central business district where the convoy took a sharp turn to the right on Cairo Road, and headed for the 50,000 capacity National Heroes Stadium located on the northern fringes of the sprawling Matero Constituency on the Great North Road.

Jubilant Lusaka residents, in their thousands, took up almost every inch either side of the three-kilometre stretch of the Great North Road from the city centre to the stadium like Christians out on Palm Sunday shouting praises and blessings to their new leader, Edgar Chagwa Lungu, as he started the long journey that would have direct impact on their daily lives for the next couple of years and even beyond.

It had been a tight contest between Edgar Lungu and Hakainde Hichilema of the United Party for National Development (UPND) and the Lusaka vote had helped to tip the balance in the PF candidate's favour by just over 27,000 votes. Hakainde Hichilema, the president of the main opposition party, the United Party for National Development (UPND), had already conceded defeat, if ever so grudgingly, in a statement on national and private radio stations in which he claimed he had been robbed of victory but without providing evidence. 'A stolen election does not reflect the will of the people,' said Hichilema's concession statement of 24 January 2015, adding, 'It is with deep regret that we now already know the predetermined result.'

While Hakainde and his supporters were left to stew and reflect over yet another electoral disappointment, PF supporters were almost unrestrained in their relief and joy at their triumph. Lungu was, after all, the local guy made good and tears of joy were not in short supply among some of those who lined the route to the venue of his inauguration.

The presidential motorcade came to a calculated, slow halt at the back entrance of the National Heroes Stadium by the full-length, swing glass doors that led to the VVIP (Very Very Important Persons) holding rooms with their immaculate snow-white leather seats and sprawling red carpets. Pure royalty.

A hustle and a shuffle, an alert security detail made a safety circle around president-elect, as they marched him into the VVIP area where he would sit and wait to be called to take the oath of office. It was so surreal, and sometimes, the whole episode looked like a 4D DVD clip straight out of a Hollywood movie scene, complete with the extras and the props, yet it was for real. Power would change hands in Zambia today, democratically, as had happened several times before since Zambia became an independent nation some fifty odd years ago.

Eventually, a retiring Edgar Lungu, standing at over six feet tall, was invited to the specially erected podium to take oath from the Acting Chief Justice Chibesakunda as crowds, captured live on television, broke into uncontrollable spasms of joyous applause. The shade over the podium was dressed in Zambian national colours: copper, green, black, and red, while its floors simply flowed in red.

Justice Chibesakunda was adorned in full ceremonial regalia. Flowing red robes and white wig, vestiges of Zambia's colonial heritage from British rule, but an important part of the mixture of pomp and solemnity that characterises such official occasions. She was about to perform the biggest task of her career—making a president.

After the routine swearing that transforms an ordinary man into a president, like the proverbial kiss from a princess that turned the frog into a prince, His Excellency Edgar Chagwa Lungu set free into the sky a white dove to more wild cheers. As the dove, that universal simile of the love and peace that Lungu pledged to stand for throughout his presidency, fluttered away, the military brass band struck up a rhythm and a continent looked on at a new dawn, a new era in one of its model democracies.

As the presidential motorcade made its way out of the stadium to take the newly installed president to his new address, the colonial-styled palatial piles on Independence Ave., complete with a golf course and resident small game, there would have been interesting conversations among the dispersing, still celebrating throng as to what kind of person they had elected into office as the sixth president of the Republic of Zambia.

Well, Lungu had given away a plethora of clues to that puzzle in a wide-ranging inauguration speech liberally sprinkled with the words love, peace, and unity and repeated references to hard work and the needs of the people, winding up his remarks words, 'As I conclude, let me state that politics is not just about winning and celebrating the victory. It is about meeting the needs and aspirations of the people, the electorate.'

President Lungu did not waste time in adding a word of caution to his colleagues in the ruling party and the government regarding the task ahead. He said, 'Let me remind my colleagues in government and the ruling party (PF) that the period before the next elections is very short. We must, therefore, work very hard in the remaining eighteen months to retain the confidence of our masters, the Zambian people. Our work starts today.' He added, 'God has been gracious to Zambia, and we pledge to honour him by adhering to Christian virtues. Zambia shall remain a Christian nation tolerant of other religions.'

The 'Christian nation' line would have reverberated right round the country, especially among Protestants who have vigorously resisted suggestions from certain quarters that the declaration be expunged from the constitution, that it served no purpose.

President Lungu closed the inauguration ceremony with a prayer, entreating God to bless the republic and concluding, 'May we always hold each other's hand and reach out and let love be at the core of all our activities. God bless you all. God Bless Zambia.'

President Lungu's message appeared to have struck a chord with the people, judging by the response it received while he delivered it as masterfully and eloquently as an old hand at the job. But then again, he had had plenty of practise addressing sell-out crowds during what had been a frenetic countrywide constituency by constituency campaign during which he had spoken mostly off the cuff.

The entire inauguration programme, from the time Edgar Lungu was driven into the stadium to the end, lasted about one hour and sixteen minutes, including the time devoted to actually reading the speech. His acceptance speech alone ran a standard, good thirty-two minutes.

Professional rules of thumb that require a speaker to spend around two minutes per page seemed to have been adhered to by Lungu's speechwriters to their credit. That placed his speech at around 3,000 words for twenty minutes and about 4,500 words for about half hour. The speech, carefully designed to 'bring out the man' and answer some pertinent questions about him, received at least twelve standing and seated ovations, as President Lungu, normally a fast speaker, delivered it in a measured, conversational manner.

All this was happening after he had received his first salute as the elected Commander-in-Chief of all armed forces in Zambia from Army Commander Lt General Paul Mihova, Zambia Air Force Commander Lt General Eric Chimese, and Zambia National Service Commandant Major-General Nathan Mulenga.

A fly-past mounted by ZAF pilots painted patterns across the sky above in Zambian national colours, while members of the 2nd Battalion of the Zambia Army, resplendent in their ceremonial dark green uniforms with glinting buttons and shiny black boots, presented arms for Lungu's first ever guard of honour as president.

The afternoon rounded off with a march-past and the traditional boom-boom of the twenty-one-gun salute echoing around the stadium. At the end of his speech, the president warned party members there would be no 'honeymoon' or victory hangover allowed to kill the development momentum set by the dearly departed founder president of the party, Michael Sata. 'This is just a curtain raiser,' he warned.

To serving members of the Sata-appointed cabinet, Lungu gave a sort of stress test. 'Tomorrow (Monday) I will hold a press conference where I will name some cabinet ministers. Some will be reappointed, others will be left out.'

The president and the first lady, Mrs Esther Lungu, whom he had earlier in his speech described as a 'true comrade and rock', then walked toward the motorcade as the ecstatic crowd, some of whom had kept vigil at the stadium from the previous day, continued to jubilate.

A South African Broadcasting Corporation (SABC) anchor, a member of the crew of one of the many local and international television companies that had joined the state-run Zambia National Broadcasting Corporation (ZNBC) to cover the event live, described President Lungu's speech as 'great'. 'It was a great speech, a well-received speech that had everything for everyone including the constitution, the economy, and jobs.'

Despite soaring afternoon temperatures, there was no thinning of the roadside crowds as the presidential motorcade headed for state house at great speed, leaving behind a waft of dust on sections of the route.

The Lungus had not yet moved into state house, partly because the new president was in no particular hurry, but also because their new home was undergoing some renovations—standard practise every time a new tenant was about to move in.

However, a traditional, ceremonial stopover at the front gate of state house directly opposite Arakan Barracks where two armed military police guards stand at attention 24/7 had to be made.

The Presidential Mercedes Benz pulled up at the gates where a sharp military salute was performed by the guards, and a trumpet sounded before the head of state was driven toward state house past the vast, salubrious grounds providing grazing for some resident impalas.

In state house, just like the ceremonial handover of the instruments of power at the National Heroes Stadium, President Lungu was shown to his office and the room where, every Monday, he would hold cabinet meetings. There was no knowing what was going through his mind as he was conducted around his new home, a far cry from his humble beginnings in Ndola where his life began on 11 November, fifty-eight years back. His ascendency to the topmost job in town had been nothing if not against all odds, for him, close friends and family.

President Edgar Lungu hosting two regional counter parts at State House in 2016. On his left, Mozambican President Filipe Nyusi and in the middle, the President of Malawi his Excellency Peter Mutharika. President Lungu and President Nyusi share a similar past. They were both Ministers of Defence before becoming Presidents of their respective countries.

President Edgar Lungu at the Levy Mwanawasa Memorial Stadium catching up on a game of soccer, Zambia's number one sport with soccer legend and one time Africa Footballer of the Year winner, Kalusha Bwalya in 2015. Kalusha led Zambia to many victories both as a player, coach and manager. He eventually propelled Zambia to a well-deserved Africa Cup Championship in February 2012. Kalusha is also the most known and perhaps respected individual outside politics.

3rd row pic 6: President Edgar Lungu is congratulated by General Ian Khama, the President of Botswana on 13th September inside the National Heroes Stadium. President Khama, a renowned fighter pilot flew himself into Lusaka, Zambia to attend President Lungu's inauguration.

President Edgar Lungu shares a light moment with South African President Jacob Zuma during a State Visit in Pretoria in November 2016.

GUY NOT SCOTT-FREE

Guy Scott, the estranged acting president of Zambia for ninety days, had survived many political mishaps starting from calling South Africans backwards to calling Tonga a 'small tribe', a very sensitive and emotive tribal epitaph in the Zambian context. Prior to that, at the height of the return to multi-party politics under late President Frederick Jacob Titus Chiluba, Scott, as Minister of Agriculture, had survived accusations of irregularly ordering the slaying of swines suspected to have contracted the killer flu. Among the thousands of animals put down were some belonging to him. He was becoming politically bulletproof, and now it looked like he could do anything he wanted and get away with it. He was the invincible man.

Scott thought he could hold his own parallel party elections complete with candidates, returning officers, observers, and candidates plus live television coverage to crown it all. Scott could write the acting chief justice and ask her to bar anyone not approved by himself, Edgar Lungu especially, from filing nominations as PF presidential candidates without his say-so, or so he thought.

He could allow choppers to fly with opposition political heads on board even after the 18:00 hours deadline had elapsed on the last day of the campaigning as stipulated by the Electoral Commission of Zambia (ECZ) even when the Zambia Air Force had refused to grant a flight permit.

He could sack Edgar Lungu from the party without blinking an eyelid or thinking about the consequences. From where they stood, Lungu's supporters in the PF and the many neutrals rooting for him, it seemed, Scott could just about do anything he wanted as the acting president, following Sata's death.

After 25 January 2015, however, Scott's world looked small as Edgar Lungu was sworn in as president of Zambia. Basically, he had been reduced to a mere shadow of the powerful man he once believed he was. Scott's proverbial political nine lives would soon come to an end, and there was absolutely nothing he could do about it. Calls for Scott's dismissal as party acting president had reached a crescendo, and yet for the longest time, no action was taken by Lungu.

Lungu was a meticulous and calculating politician who always took his time before taking any serious decision, interrogating the consequences of his actions before finally nailing it. Something he could have picked out of law or military school or maybe it came naturally for him.

In the Scott case, Lungu, yet again, did not want to act in haste or take any decision that might be misinterpreted as revenge. Given the hostility, he had suffered at the hands of Scott in his quest for the presidency. Lungu would have been regarded as perfectly in order had he openly denounced and sacked his former boss.

Instead, President Lungu offered him a job as Minister of Commerce and Industry, a very crucial position in cabinet, and for which he seemed particularly well suited given his qualifications in economics and deep understanding of the issues affecting the country on this front.

Scott asked for a day to think about the offer and returned with a counter-proposal. He would take the post of Minister of Tourism. At this point, Lungu made the decision to let Scott go, deciding it was in the best interest of all concerned; himself, Scott, and more importantly, the party.

The Daily Nation Newspaper (published by former State House Press Aide to President Chiluba, Richard Sakala) appeared more than any other Zambian publication, to relish Scott's exit, which they interpreted as a dismissal. The Daily Nation's masthead story described how one of Lungu's first major action as president was to replace Scott with Zambia's first female vice president, Inonge Wina.

Below is the full Daily Nation article:

'President Edgar Lungu has dropped Guy Scott as vice president of Zambia, and has replaced him with Inonge Wina, who becomes the first female vice president since Zambia attained her independence in 1964.

'When the Daily Nation phoned Scott to ask what he thought of the development, parting company with President Lungu, Scott refused to speak to the newspaper, saying, "*Imwe baba simumvela chizungu* (You, sir, do not understand English). No comment, no comment, no comment!" Scott said before cutting the line.'

President Lungu chose, as he had done many times before when confronted with the issue of Guy Scott, not to discuss his former boss, but took time, once again, to extoll the many virtues of the solid Mrs Wina, her wisdom, and courage that had helped to hold the party together at its most trying moments during the succession wrangles that emerged after the death of President Sata.

Mrs Wina has a rich educational and professional background with a number of degrees behind her name including in History and Sociology, apart from being a social worker. 'I want to say something about the vice president. She is a solid woman who stood firm when we faced possible disintegration. I pay tribute to her for her courage during the time we were going through turbulence,' President Lungu said.

And with those words, Guy Scott was history, at least as far as the party he had helped to found was concerned.

EDGAR IN THE EYES OF 'QUEEN' ESTHER

Esther Nyawa Lungu, First Lady of the Republic of Zambia, was born on 2 June 1957 to parents, Island and Agnes Phiri. Mrs Lungu is a woman well known for her good deeds. Notable have been her attempts to uplift the livelihoods of girls and vulnerable women. Also, in such acts as simply mourning with and otherwise showing solidarity with ordinary Zambians in trying times.

On the face of it, such acts seem ordinary and inconsequential, but these do, in fact, resonate very deeply with large sections of the Zambian society, fully endorsing the first lady as a mother figure and accentuating her respectability.

Apart from the President's late parents, Tasila and Padule Lungu, Esther, his wife of thirty plus years, is the only other person who can be said to truly know Edgar Lungu. Not only is she almost always the first person to see him when he wakes, and last before he goes to sleep, but she is probably the only person who fully understands the depth of his ambition, the passions that drive him, and what lengths he will go to in order to protect his personal interests.

During one media interview, Esther gave the nation a rare insight into the 'softer side' of Zambia's silent, but steely commander-in-chief and sixth president, describing him as a 'kind and loving man', who, among other things, dislikes all forms of segregation and is deeply devoted to his family. Said Esther of awisi (father of) Daliso, 'You may know him as the president or the commander-in-chief, but to me, he is just Edgar, a very loving and kind man whose heart bleeds whenever he encounters human suffering, and in his line of work, there is a lot of it. He strives to have a just Zambia in the midst of huge challenges, and I greatly admire him for that. Edgar is a great dad and fantastic granddad too. Since he became the sixth president of Zambia on 25 January 2015, he has remained my same loving and caring husband who, despite his busy schedule, has continued to make a little time for his old friends, as well as making new ones with the same old Edgar Lungu ease. He also has a lot of time to listen to both sides of the story before making a decision, and his judgement call is often on point. He does not rush decisions. I think it's because he knows the impact his decisions might have on people and indeed the country.'

Mrs Lungu reckons the president's humble beginnings in the poverty-stricken Chimwemwe Township of Kitwe, combined with a deeply religious upbringing, underpin his deep empathy for and generosity toward the underprivileged. The first family is staunch Baptists, albeit Edgar's United Church of Zambia (UCZ) roots. Mrs Lungu herself was initially a Roman Catholic. Given that background, it is not surprising that she continues to bask in what is perhaps the highest point in her religious life—President and Mrs Lungu's meeting with the Pope at the Vatican.

How did the first family become Baptists? Mrs Lungu relates how when the couple first met Edgar had his UCZ hymn books, while she had her Catholic catechism books—in short, each one was practising a different doctrine. They decided on a compromise in the Baptist Church. 'Christianity', says Mrs Lungu, 'is something very dear to Edgar's heart. It is perhaps why I love him so much. He hates injustice, and he takes his God and saviour, Jesus Christ, very seriously in all his work. He believes in equality for all regardless of tribe or gender.'

As to the first family status, Mrs Lungu states that the presidency came rather as a surprise. For her, this further testimony that leadership comes from God, and in her view, her husband's presidency was conferred by God; the Zambian people voted for her husband because the good Lord led them to believe that he was a good and just man.

'I personally never tire to thank God for the blessings he has given my husband, the blessings my husband passes to the nation selflessly and tirelessly,' she says. It is this 'selfless service', which Esther Lungu says, is the inspiration for her voluntary work in the community. She says, 'Edgar has a tough and lonely job, but I want to make sure that the family helps him out as much as possible.' This she does by participating in unpaid community service.

The first lady recalls how tough it was when the family first moved into state house and were suddenly thrust into the local and international spotlight. Mrs Lungu talks of the challenges faced by her husband suddenly finding himself at the helm. She recalls that the nation's hospitals were low on medicines and other supplies. There was a climate change induced drought; and a shortage of fuel and electricity, among other tests, which Edgar had to immediately grapple with.

According to his wife, Edgar took all these in stride, 'He was president from day one,' she gushes with pride. Specific developments included his consent to a draft constitution that had been the source of much debate and friction between various political players and civil society, the continuation of an infrastructure development programme (unprecedented since independence), and the investment of over 4 billion US dollars in the energy sector, which had been neglected for more than forty years.

Mrs Lungu asserts, 'I think my husband has, under quite harsh circumstances, done a commendable job, and I believe he will do even better once he is given a full five-year mandate instead of just a year and half. I am a mother, and I know that it is practically impossible to achieve much in a year even a child is barely functional in a year.'

On a personal level, Esther recalls 9 March 2015 as one of the darkest days in her life. Just over a month after Edgar's swearing-in as state president, he was at Heroes Stadium on International Women's Day performing one of his first national duties when he became breathless and collapsed. Official cause was extreme exhaustion following a gruelling non-stop campaign that saw him cross the country until the day he was sworn into office. Esther was not alone in her fears. The whole country was apprehensive, having just recently buried President Michael Sata, the second president to die in office after Levy Mwanawasa.

Esther, ever the devout Christian, knelt down and prayed to God when her husband collapsed. The incident proved to be a blessing in disguise to the Lungus in that the resultant battery of tests revealed dangerous levels of lifestyle related fragility, which if not discovered and addressed at the time, would have seriously compromised the president's health in very short order.

Mrs Lungu called the March incident God-sent. Because of that, she now 'takes special care' what her husband eats or drinks, including what time he goes to sleep and wakes up. Not only is Esther her husband's chief dietician and schedule manager, but she is also his wardrobe manager. She must be doing something right. Edgar Lungu has been described in some circles as 'Zambia's best dressed president' to date.

At this, Mrs Lungu gushes with pride, and then in typical Zambian matronly fashion, proceeds to offer advice to young women to 'take very good care of their husbands, and young husbands to take very good care of their wives'. In the words of his wife, Esther, Edgar is a simple man with simple tastes in food and in dress. Esther describes herself as a simple woman whose job it is at the moment to ensure as normal a home life as possible for the president.

'When he gets home and takes off his presidential jacket, he chats with everyone, plays with his grandchildren, and gives fatherly counsel to his children,' she says. There was of course, no doubt who Mrs Lungu would be voting for in the 11 August 2016 elections along with the rest of the family because 'he has a big heart, he is a tested leader, and a God-fearing, humble, but also a tough man,' says the first lady.

A Prince Is Born

As he assumed ever more responsibilities under Michael Sata's presidency, the most frequently asked question in Zambian politics soon became 'Who is Edgar Chagwa Lungu?' Those who knew Lungu before his involvement in politics recall him as the lanky lawyer who was a partner at the downtown Andre Masiye and Company law firm in Lusaka. Others would describe him as an easy-going fellow, a lawyer in whose company you felt instantly at ease even if you were only meeting him for the first time. It's the reason he was so well-loved among his constituents of Chawama.

But Lungu was also capable of going it alone as campaigner for what he believed in. By the time he was cutting his political teeth, he had decided that the court room was not big enough for him to change ordinary peoples' lives, but he was not always a politician.

He started out in the corporate world working as a lawyer for Barclays Bank Plc and the mining Conglomerate, ZCCM. This was after doing his obligatory stint with the Government of the Republic of Zambia upon his graduation from UNZA in 1981, and having been called to the Bar in 1983. Interestingly, his career started at the Ministry of Justice where he worked as a rookie lawyer. It was here, that by a twist of fate or faith, he would later serve as minister, in one of his earlier government portfolios.

Though little known before 2011, Lungu is many things to many people. By 2011 and 2012, the name Edgar Chagwa Lungu, when it was spoken, and it was often spoken, evoked all sorts of emotions. This, of course, depended on where, whether in a business office, church, diplomatic circles, the opposition, or just a chat over a cup of tea or coffee in Zambia.

Lungu, or simply 'Ba Edigar', as he used to be known (before becoming president of Zambia) by friends and enemies alike, is a quiet unpretentious man. However, he is not shy to give a well-considered opinion on issues, whether controversial or not, as long as he feels competent enough to do so.

For instance, some will recall vividly how, when the 'tolerance' (to gay rights) gospel was first preached, and African leaders seemed to be capitulating in order to qualify for aid that he was one of those who told the west in very blunt terms not to try to impose homosexual beliefs on Zambians. His exact words during a BBC interview ahead of the 2015 polls were, 'It (the gayism) is repugnant to my people, and I would not impose it on them because it is not their culture.' He went on to say, 'I won't touch that subject with a five-metre bamboo pole.'

Party insiders will also recall him standing up on sensitive issues in the ruling Patriotic Front (PF). One incident relates to a deeply divisive issue in October 2013 when a rift emerged as the Wynter Kabimba Guy Scott 'Cartel' camp called other party members tribal and corrupt.

Calling for unity of purpose, Lungu told the Kabimba camp, 'You cannot run with the fox and hunt with the hounds. If we are dirty and corrupt then you must leave us and form your own organisation which is non-tribal and plays clean politics.'

Such was Lungu's galvanising effect on his fellow PF members. His leadership capabilities were progressively acknowledged even before he assumed senior leadership within the party, and later on, the party presidency and national presidency. If we may step back a little in time, by the time of the Levy Mwanawasa presidency in 2001, ordinary citizens were becoming more and more disenchanted after ten years of the MMD.

Cracks had begun to appear in the political façade, as by the early 2000s, the party was no longer celebrated as the liberator from the authoritarian UNIP. The MMD had taken on its own demons, and was now increasingly associated with high-level graft, rigged elections, even alleged murderous plots against political opponents. As if that was not enough, the party's leader and national president, Frederick Chiluba, was seeking an unconstitutional third term in office, infuriating Zambians even more.

The political atmosphere was highly charged. Plural politics had brought with it certain liberties, and free speech was being exercised in all quarters from the press to individuals. Civil society was up in arms, agitating for accountability from policy-makers. New political parties were popping up as politicians, whose aspirations were not being met by the major parties, left to pursue their agendas in new organisations.

In the meantime, almost every Zambian had become a politician in their own rights. They practised their politics by calling radio stations (even giving their real names) during live radio broadcasts to express usually unflattering opinions on the ruling party and government. People also exercised their freedom, moving from one political party to another, or attending political rallies en masse. Lungu, for his part, had briefly joined the UPND. However, he quickly ditched it, moving to Sata's recently formed and virtually untested PF.

Somehow, Lungu's sixth lawyer's sense told him that Sata, already a household name and grassroots organiser in his own right, had more political aptitude than any other leader in the country at the time. If anyone could amass enough support for the 'change' agenda, it was Sata. Lungu bade farewell to the UPND and its glamorous leadership, saying, 'In politics, you need a proper mix of politicians and managers, which is what I find in the Patriotic Front under President Sata.'

When Lungu was leaving the UPND, it appeared to his cynics to be the welcome case of 'trash taking itself out' and 'good riddance'. However, he remained unruffled. He followed Sata when, given the atmosphere at the time, it really was not the most fashionable thing to do. Lungu had early on proved himself to be a man with foresight. 'He was not your regular Joe that just read the books and stayed in class. He hang out and mingled with other students across the tribal and social status. It did not matter to Lungu,' says Boniface Chimbwali, a long-time friend of Lungu's who, at the time of publication of this book, was permanent secretary for Luapula Province.

THE LUNGU FORESIGHT

Edgar Lungu's uncanny foresight probably explains why when many young folk his age were doing everything possible to avoid compulsory military training at the Zambia National Service (ZNS), he went the whole nine yards and even signed up for more. This was to hold him in very good stead later in life, when he served as Defence Minister, and effective boss of the entire military services, and commander-in-chief.

The ZNS had been imported by the UNIP Government from Eastern Europe for the purpose of preparing the country to defend itself from the threat posed by Apartheid South Africa and Ian Smith's Southern Rhodesia. Zambian youths, upon completion of their secondary school, were required to undertake no less than six months of mandatory military training. The whole programme lasted from 1974 to 1982, being good in principle, but proving to be a financial and implementation disaster before it was given the boot.

Lungu went beyond his obligatory six months, going on to undertake a more gruelling physical and mental training stint at what is called the 'West Point' of Zambia, the military establishment of Zambia or MILTEZ in Kabwe. The training is intense. It involves breaking down minnows and turning them into men, soldiers, who might in the future, be called upon to defend their country in the old fashioned way. Lungu still vividly recalls brothers-in-arms and friendships forged during those months of arduous training and physical hardship.

One of those was Joe Chilaizya, Zambia's current Deputy Ambassador to the United States, who had also served as Director General of the Zambia National Broadcasting Corporation (ZNBC). Chilaizya had gone on from the military to pursue journalism.

Lungu himself had taken a journalism course, and another in teaching. However, his heart was always with law, which was where it eventually drove him—away from the media and the men in uniform. Prominent Lusaka lawyer, Kelvin Bwalya Fube, says that perhaps it is this rare mix of the law and military discipline that enabled Lungu to get along so well with the rather complicated collection of paradoxes the made up the man called Sata.

The late president's affection for Lungu had become increasingly evident when on several recorded 'Let the People Talk' radio interviews, Sata was often heard to mention Lungu alone by name, saying, 'I would like to thank my lawyer Edgar Lungu, and everyone (else) working with us.' This perhaps went as far back as 2002 when Sata's dream to become president was just that of a dream.

Lungu's Recipe for Success

How far has Lungu's political career been influenced by his legal past or trappings? Students of leadership reckon there is a strong magnetic force that draws lawyers to politics. Could this be the same force that seems to have set Lungu on his current career path of public service? Indeed, it has also been observed that in democracies within and outside Africa, lawyers seem to dominate the political scene, as can be witnessed from Washington to Paris to London. Perhaps this is due to the fact that the law, more often than not, addresses the same sorts of issues, as do politics—issues of right and wrong, justice and injustices.

For instance, lawyers often have to deal with the hard facts of what makes a just society. The balance between liberty and security, between right and wrong, as well as navigating other more grey areas in day-to-day life. Legal skills have also been understood to enable the marshalling of evidence, appealing to juries and procedural issues, which are easily transferred to the political stage.

Many political thinkers link lawyers like Edgar Lungu to power and politics, and maintain that lawyers make natural leaders because of their obsession with processes and a tendency to see things in non-partisan 'us against them', and 'guilty or not guilty'.

It is also generally believed that any lawyer worth his or her salt will often be driven by the spirit of loyalty to a cause above the lure of money, a quality which is rare in other professions such as the business profession.

Lungu is not the first Zambian lawyer to take political centre stage. Levy Mwanawasa, the third president of Zambia, can be credited with having set the tone, following the re-introduction of multiparty politics in 1991 when he served as vice president and eventually president. Otherwise thus far, Zambia has seen a mixed cast, including freedom fighters, a trade unionist, and two career politicians. As the country's political history is still being written, it remains to be seen, which other lawyers will take up the presidential challenge following in the footsteps of Lungu and Mwanawasa.

Elsewhere, in democracies abroad, lawyers' names abound in politics. This is especially notable in the United States of America, where at a certain point in its political history, President Barak Obama, the first African American President, was thus far the twenty-fifth lawyer to serve as the president of the United States of America.

In France, studies confirm nine of Nicolas Sarkozy's first cabinet were lawyers. In Francois Hollande's government, sixteen were either lawyers or law graduates, including the president himself, the prime minister, and the finance minister.

As is the case with many lawyers, having a long career under their belt, Edgar Lungu's legal victories over his thirty plus year career have been many and varied. Perhaps it was the lawyer in him that enabled Lungu to avert in 2013, the escalation of a knotty spat into an even messier affair pitting the Football Association of Zambia (FAZ) and the Democratic Republic of Congo's top football club, TP Mazembe, over three Zambian internationals employed by the four-time African club champions.

Rainford Kalaba, Stopilla Nsunzu, and Nathan Sinkala's passports had been withheld by the Zambian Immigration Department for having left the country without proper immigration clearance on an earlier occasion, apparently on FAZ orders. Without their passports, the footballers, all members of the squad that had won the 2012 Africa Cup of Nations, could not report for duty at the DRC Club, which had forked out some serious money for their services. Needless to say, TP Mazembe officials led by club president, Moise Katumbi, then governor of the mineral-rich Katanga province, were not very impressed. Amidst a welter of accusations and counter-accusations over who did what, when, and why feeding the sports pages of newspapers in both countries, Lungu quickly stepped in to nip a potentially explosive situation in the bud.

As Minister of Home Affairs then, Lungu quickly established that there was, in fact, nothing grievously or galactically illegal about a Zambian leaving the country without the appropriate endorsement in their passport by the Immigration Department. To his devoted 'nay-sayers' who considered it their duty to question his wisdom, Lungu made reference to the footballers' role in the February 2012 Africa Cup triumph–Zambia's first ever in over fifty years of trying. Lungu told his critics and those of the boys, 'Just a couple of months ago, these boys united the country and put Zambia on the world map as a great footballing nation. They were true heroes, and yet today, someone wants to treat them like criminals. I don't think it's right. Give them back their passports.'

It was not the first time Lungu was getting involved in resolving a football-related controversy. Were it not for the tireless efforts of his law firm working in tandem with another one, the long-running compensation saga relating to the 1993 plane crash that claimed the lives of an entire travelling party of thirty, among them eighteen Zambian internationals, after the plane carrying them to a World Cup qualifying match in Senegal went down off the Atlantic coast of Gabon, would have gone on for longer still.

The case was becoming an embarrassment to successive governments for their failure to help both the grieving families and the soccer fraternity to put closure to one of the saddest chapters in Zambian football history. Lungu teamed up with colleague, prominent Lusaka lawyer, Sakwiba Sikota, to pressure the government to pay up the compensation package. A hefty K16 billion in old money, demanded by the families of those smothered in the tragedy.

Twenty-two years on from the disaster, the January 2014 issue of the Richard Sakala Daily Nation newspaper quotes a widow of one the victims of the crash expressing her personal gratitude to Lungu, telling of how she and her family had remained 'eternally grateful to Mr Lungu for his personal effort to secure our payment when he was not getting anything (lawyer fees) out of the case,' the widow said. 'We would have never been compensated for the loss had it not been for the efforts of Honourable Lungu who was then a lawyer in private practise.'

In fact, it had taken eleven years and two presidents (Frederick Jacob Titus Chiluba and Levy Mwanawasa) for Lungu and Sakwiba Sikota to finally unlock, on behalf of the Gabon Disaster victim's relatives the money which was distributed equally among the families. No doubt this deed elevated Lungu in the estimation of many ordinary Zambians. Some Gabon payout recipients describe Lungu as an 'honourable man with nothing but good intentions, a great lawyer indeed who deserves all the respect and love he is currently getting.'

Leah Sakala, aged thirty now, was only 5 years old when her father, Corporal Thomson Sakala, one of the crew of the fated military plane carrying the national team to Senegal went down. Leah, who could not have had much awareness of the legal battle raging on her behalf until much later in life, enthuses, 'Mr Lungu is a good man.'

Lungu, ever shy of taking credit has reluctantly confirmed using his own money to fight for the compensation of the Gabon disaster families, for the loss of their loved ones, while closely working with Sakwiba Sikota.

Indeed, Lungu was known to frequently dip into his own pocket to help with transport, at times even food, as representatives of the 'Gabon families', as the media refers to them, regularly traversed between their homes and the two lawyers' offices.

In their casting about for someone, anyone, to help, the lines were understandably blurred for the desperate families. In the meantime, the case dragged on at quite an expense in form of money and time.

For his part, comprehending the difficulties that the grieving families were facing, Lungu never complained. His focus was instead on the big prize—justice in the form of monetary compensation for the relatives, and the opportunity to help them put closure to the case. 'I knew the money, when it would finally come, would cushion the hardships the families had gone through after the untimely loss of their relatives,' Lungu says. 'But then, in the back of my mind, I also knew that no amount of money could ever take the place of their beloved lost ones. You cannot attach a price to a human life', Lungu mused.

'At the expense of sounding repetitive, I would say a human life is priceless'.

MEET DEPUTY MINISTER EDGAR LUNGU

When finally in government, in 2011 after Sata's PF unseated the Rupiah Banda-led MMD, Lungu did not go straight into an influential ministerial portfolio, but started off as a junior minister in the vice president's office, Guy Scott being the vice president then. Unlike some of his colleagues who appeared to always hit the ground at a steady trot, Lungu seemed to always be starting off from the bottom of the barrel. This was true of both party, and later on, government positions. In fact, the most striking thing about Lungu's early political life is that he was never a 'front runner'.

One example is that of his quest for the Chawama Constituency seat as MP.

Lungu was touched by the ubiquitous poverty and squalor of Chawama Compound, home to a number of his friends and relatives.

Being the crusader that he is, he took up the cause of doing something to improve the lives of the township's residents. It was not long before he concluded that improving people's lives could best be achieved by political means, hence, his application for adoption as the PF parliamentary candidate in 2006.

Sata passed Lungu over for Reverend Sampa-Bredt (now deceased), but Lungu did not sulk or threaten to quit. He remained an ordinary PF member taking up every chore Sata gave him without as much as a grudge. This was the beginning of the next phase of Lungu's life—that of a politician.

Lungu already enjoyed considerable support from within the party, not to mention his substantial grassroots contacts arising from a legal career spanning close to thirty years. To ordinary mortals in the PF, all indications were that he was a natural contender for Chawama. However, PF President Sata did not quite see it that way. Since no one dared question the Cobra, Lungu's ambitions for Chawama had to be put on hold. However, there was a change years later in 2011, with Lungu now a little more influential within the party, and now even better known within the community. 'In 2011, the same seat was available, and this time, I was allowed to stand. I won the seat after a lot of hardcore campaigning,' Lungu states in an interview taped for the SABC in Pretoria in February 2015.

After rather unremarkable beginnings Lungu's meteoric rise from political insignificance was now well underway. He was now in phase II of his political career. Phase I, consisting of mere political party membership and twice unsuccessfully bidding for the Chawama seat, had been in danger of ending up the way many others' attempts at politics have ended up, in 'truncated political development'.

Commenting on Lungu's later successes, Lusaka lawyer, KBF, who is also a close friend and unabashed supporter, said, 'Many politicians, especially those without stamina, chutzpah, or ideology, and above all, loyalty would have given up at the first loss and subsequent rejection, but Edgar, the president now, didn't. He stayed on, bided his time, listened to the party leadership's call for restraint, remained loyal, and above all, patient—a true mark of leadership and unquestionable resilience if you ask me.'

House number 4001 in Chimwemwe Township in the mining town of Kitwe where President Edgar Lungu started his humble beginnings before becoming a successful lawyer and eventually the sixth President of Zambia.

President Edgar Lungu is flanked by Democratic Republic of Congo (DRC) President Laurent Kabila and President Eduardo dos Santos of Angola at an international event.

President Edgar Lungu addresses the Southern African Development Community
(SADC) heads of states in Gaborone, Botswana in August 2015.

THE SATA-LUNGU CONNECTION

In September 2011, Michael Chilufya Sata made history. He, an opposition candidate, and himself a study in resilience and political stamina, had succeeded in democratically unseating a serving government with still five years to go on its tenure.

It was a noteworthy achievement given the fact that in Africa, barring a revolution, this is an extremely rare occurrence.

For Zambia, this was only the second time such a thing was happening, the first being the unforgettable, epochal change from one-party tyranny under Kenneth Kaunda's UNIP to multi-party rule under the MMD in 1991.

It should be considered, though, that the defeat of Kaunda's UNIP by the MMD's flamboyant, gospel-preaching, Bible-quoting, tongue-speaking Frederick Jacob Titus Chiluba was nothing short of a revolution.

In the words of political pundit H. L. Mencken, 'Under a democracy, one party always devotes its chief energies to trying to prove that the other party is unfit to rule — and both commonly succeed, and are right.'

Lungu, it seemed, had been crowded out of a better, more deserving role (full cabinet minister) by individuals 'coming from behind' such as Chongwe legislator Sylvia Masebo and Wynter Kabimba that once belonged to an obscure opposition party.

However, in June 2012, Lungu got his big break: in what some political commentators have described as the fastest rise in political office, President Sata elevated him to the highly influential position of Home Affairs Minister. The timing of this move was notable, for this early in PF's rule, fissures had started to appear, as intra-party differences began to manifest themselves.

In the meantime, Lungu's dramatic rise in the ranks from a hugely ignored political light-weight to Home Affairs Minister had catapulted him into the harsh media spot-light, exposing him to the most unforgiving and even scathing scrutiny.

The now publicly visible Lungu had become the target of vicious attacks from all sections of the media, including print, on-line and broadcast that was mostly opposition-inclined.

It has been suggested that these attacks were instigated by players from within political circles, special interest power brokers, including some supposed colleagues, who were working in collusion with certain media personalities to discredit Lungu. The idea was to stop him in his walking tracks before he could walk.

They were apparently uncomfortable with his public boldness, which they themselves were incapable of due, perhaps, to the many skeletons in their proverbial closets. However, no matter how malicious the attacks, Lungu always chose not to respond.

Instead, he piled up the responsibilities on Lungu. At the time of Satas' passing, Lungu held no fewer than five high ranking titles, the man of many hats, with the ruling party the PF, and government. Not bad for man the opposition media like to call a slouch or plain visionless.

When once or twice he was forced to respond to the constant stream of disparaging, inflammatory and even defamatory criticism of himself, Lungu had the following answer: 'Let them have their say, we shall have our way...we have been given a huge responsibility to serve the people under President Sata and that duty is sacred. We cannot waste time responding to each media report because there will be no time to work.'

Lungu had clearly read the Robert Greene's famous '48 Laws of Power', one of the most profound rule that states in part: '....but a human tongue is a beast that few can master. It strains to constantly break out of its cage, and if (it's) not tame (d), it would turn wild and cause you grief.'

Meanwhile, as the attacks against Lungu mounted, he simply developed a thick skin. It was as if he knew that the media torrent was a plan by his detractors to make him lose sight of his duty to national service.

Zambians were watching, as were curious local and foreign media, who wondered where the wind would blow, for the 'officer, lawyer and gentleman.'

Notwithstanding, the blitz of negative press against Lungu, Sata surprised many in Zambia in his acknowledgement of Lungu by promoting him (Lungu) to the very powerful post of Minister of Defence, a much-coveted position, just recently vacated by Godfrey Bwalya Mwamba (GBM), who had quit the PF party in frustration.

As Defence Minister, Lungu was now, by hierarchy, the fourth most powerful politician in Zambia, (fresh out of the Ministry of Home Affairs) and still the Disciplinary Committee chair in the ruling PF, an unpopular position given that it have the office holder sometimes had to discipline even close colleagues in the interest of the greater good of the party and nation.

Without raising the obvious questions about whether Lungu was not a little over-taxed by all these duties, it was by now evident to all that the visibly ailing Sata had come to rely more and more on his younger confidante.

Lungu's role was increasingly that of a trusted ally and buffer in a sea of hungry political wolves. When pointedly asked why he continued to 'over-load' Lungu with more responsibilities, President Sata is quoted as having told a confidante: 'That young man Edgar Lungu has a good heart…he can take care of people and unite them.' This was of course delivered in the President's favourite language, Bemba: 'Ulya mwana Edgar Lungu ali kwata umutima uusuma sana . . . kuti asangu bwino abantu'.

If Lungu felt overloaded by the growing weight of responsibility on his shoulders, he didn't complain, at least not publicly. In fact, his customary response both privately and publicly, was something to the rather immodest effect that he was 'equal to the task.'

In one of his comments upon being appointed Defence Minister, Lungu is quoted as saying, characteristically: 'I shall continue to pledge my loyalty to President Sata who has given me all these rare opportunities and I will continue being a team player.'

He repeated this message during his first interview as President of Zambia with SABC in South Africa in South Africa where he had travelled to receive medical attention in March after an unfortunate collapsing incident on International Women's Day at Heroes Stadium on 8th March 2015, barely two months after assuming office. This part (collapsing) is discussed in detail by the First Lady Esther Nyawa Lungu.

It would appear that none of his numerous titles made Lungu one bit big-headed or self-conceited, as the case was for instance with others before him. Even with the 'many hats' that he had on, he continued to display the same unassuming character he had when only a junior minister under Vice President, Guy Scott.

COURAGE UNDER FIRE

Lungu was the Minister of Defence when on 14 May 2014, tragedy struck the Zambian Military. Zambia Air Force (ZAF) Deputy Commander, Major General Muliokela Muliokela, and Air Force Colonel Brian Mweene, were killed when their plane crashed in the Lusaka West Farming area during routine training. As Minister of Defence, Lungu was tasked with the responsibility of instituting and managing a probe into the unfortunate loss of highly decorated senior ZAF officers. Lungu also had to deal with the resultant media frenzy, for as tragic as a plane crash can be when it involves fatalities, it is a matter of intense interest from local media, as it would be anywhere else in the world, especially when the military is involved.

Confirming the accident on the national broadcaster, Defence Minister Edgar Lungu said, 'It is with a heavy heart and a lot of regret that I inform the public that today, between 12:30 hours and 13:30 hours, a ZAF aircraft was involved in an accident, killing both pilots on board. Investigations have been instituted into the matter to establish the cause.'

A probe into the crash ensued, overseen by, and in consultation with, the ZAF Air Commander, Lieutenant General Eric Chimese, a vibrant and youthful air commander who also chaired the Joint Military Committee of the Zambian Military. He was deputised by Major General David Muma. The make of the plane was Swedish made trainer Saab MS 15.

Edgar had in the past ridden or flown on the plane similar to the one that had crashed. The two officers were buried at Memorial Park with full military honours.

Lungu: Man of the People

In the meantime, Lungu continued with what had become his daily routine. At the end of a normal workday, Lungu would knock off either from the Ministry of Defence or from parliament building, and head south of Lusaka to visit his constituency. Here, Lungu was something of a high priest, deity, rock star, and counsellor, all rolled into one. Any day he set out to visit his constituency, there was no knowing what he might be called upon to do that day.

His roles extended from mediating in marital disagreements and other sorts of personal disputes to checking on the construction of a health post, police post, or road project. Here was where he first cut his political teeth, and he was not letting any constituent down no matter how confused or complicated their expectations.

As frequently as he would be asked about his devotion to his constituency, Lungu would respond, 'The people of Chawama are my employers. I would not be a cabinet minister without them. I need to stay in touch with them so that I do not lose touch of why I am privileged to serve in this government.' Then, as if to reaffirm his resolve, he would add, 'Whatever happens, whatever the good Lord throws on to you in terms of privilege, do not forget those that are less privileged than you are because God gives and takes. Today, you are a minister, tomorrow you are a nobody.'

He recognised from the very beginning that keeping it real was perhaps more important than growing wings or horns as a public leader, or indeed any other person that sought to lead others. Whatever may be said or written about Lungu, the one thing that stands out about his character is his ability to bring himself down to the level of, and connect with the less privileged, the proletariat class as it were.

Perhaps he is a product of his own humble beginnings, or perhaps it comes from his deep religious upbringing. 'Lungu appears to have learnt and embraced loyalty at a very early stage in his upbringing socially and as a law student,' KBF once analysed. But as seen from the account of the Gabon widows, Lungu's encounters with the less fortunate seem to always be filled with empathy and respect.

One young lawyer working under Lungu recalls how once, as he walked into the court premises, Lungu turned to him and asked whether he had said hello 'to that good old woman'. Looking around in puzzlement, the protégé said, 'Which woman, sir?'

As Lungu pointed at the cleaning woman who, by the young protégé's own admission, had been invisible to him until Lungu pointed him her direction and said, 'Learn to say hello to these great but simple people. Learn their names and they will learn yours because they are good people, and their duties are invaluable though largely unrecognised.'

Well, Lungu's disposition has proved a useful asset to him. Any time he goes on the campaign trail, he has no difficulty being all things to all people.

An interesting anecdote relates to an interview, which Lungu had in late December 2013, with a Zambia Daily Mail journalist who called him asking for this take on the ending of 2013 as a year in politics. The then Minister of Home Affairs said, 'A day in a politician's life is too long, my friend. I cannot competently sum up 2013 today before the year actually ends because we just don't know, as politicians, what happens the next day.'

The next day, Lungu was appointed Minister of Defence, in addition to his numerous other responsibilities as a member of the PF supreme council, the central committee. In accepting this new appointment, the usual Lungu humility kicked in as he stated, 'It is a remarkable honour for me. I feel humbled by the magnitude of the responsibility bestowed upon me by the president to serve the people of Zambia.' By now, it had to be obvious to almost everyone within PF that Lungu's star was on the rise, and that nothing was going to slow him down. He had already been bestowed the rare privilege of acting as president of Zambia in Sata's absence twice.

Somehow, unlike others that had acted, when Lungu was left with the instruments of power, there was no uproar, as the case would be the one time that Kabimba, would act. In fact, oftentimes than not, no matter how short the period would be, Lungu used his executive powers to help one institution or another by exerting muscle in the right direction.

The Zambia Daily Mail, for instance, was a struggling public-owned newspaper with low readership numbers of about 5,000 copies nationally on a daily basis, and huge uncollected advertising revenues owed to it by the government over years.

In 2012, when Edgar Lungu was on his acting presidency duties, working closely and directly with this author (then Deputy Managing Director of the Zambia Daily Mail) helped the newspaper recover up to five billion Kwacha (old currency) about US$1million. The money, owed over years, was recovered within one week by Mukwita and Lungu. It is correct to say the newspaper's current path to success has Lungu written somewhere on it.

KALUSHA AND THE
WINNING TEAM

As Lungu's campaign machine lapped up the miles around the country in the last weeks before the 11 August 2016 elections, he was frequently joined on the stage by an ever-growing assemblage of local celebrities, mostly musicians and comedians, lending their talents to his cause. They would be joined later by the one person whose star would outshine them all— Kalusha Bwalya, Zambia's internationally celebrated footballer.

The ex-Zambia captain and 1988 African footballer of the year award winner was warmly greeted wherever he stood to speak, often with a football under that bewitching left foot of his that had been the bane of defenders across the four continents where he wrought his magic as an attacking midfielder.

At almost all of Edgar Lungu's political rallies, about two months before the polls, Kalusha was invited to speak for Lungu and the Lungu team. Kalusha, who had also served as coach of Zambia before moving up to become president of the local FA, drew from vast experience in the game—on the field and off it. 'Football wisdom tells you never to change a winning team. The PF and President Edgar Lungu has proved itself a winning team from its performance since coming to power,' he said at one meeting. 'I know what a winning team looks like. I've never backed a loser,' he said at another.

Kalusha's appeal to the voters on behalf of Lungu was based on his own first-hand experiences of the candidate's empathetic involvement in helping to resolve the compensation claims of the surviving families of his Zambia teammates that died in a tragic plane crash that claimed the lives of all thirty passengers on board when the aircraft went down off the Gabonese Coast as the party made its way to Senegal to fulfill a 1994 World Cup qualifier.

As captain of the team, and saved only by the fact that he was based in Europe at the time, Kalusha was almost as personally affected by the tragedy as the families themselves. Some of the players who perished in the crash like the long-serving keeper, Efford Chabala, were people he had known for years, played alongside early in his career at Mufulira Wanderers, and even shared a room on their travels. Many others like Patrick 'Bomber' Banda, Kenan Simambe, Kelvin Mutale, and Numba Mwila were up-and-coming youngsters sizzling with talent that was being lauded as the most outstanding of its generation with Kalusha providing the inspiration and guidance needed for them to fulfill their potential. The two coaches killed on that night of 28 April 1993, Godfrey 'Ucar' Chitalu and Alex Chola, ranked among his own inspirations as a budding footballer.

As Kalusha repeated many times during those dark days when a grieving nation grappled with coming to terms with such a huge loss, a part of his family had been torn away from him and from Zambian football fraternity forever.

While rebuilding the team would resume within months, with Zambia defying the odds and making the finals of the 1994 African final, and just falling at the last hurdle in the quest to make the FIFA World Cup finals held later that year in the USA, there would be no short-circuiting the healing process for the bereaved families. They had lost fathers, husbands, breadwinners, sons, uncles, and brothers who were pillars in their families.

With time, though, the initial outpouring of sympathy for the 'Gabon families', as they would be referred to in the media, would turn into impatience as the compensation claims began to assume a rather nasty tone with allegations that the government and the nation were being insensitive to their plight.

Enter Edgar Lungu

It was at this point that Edgar Lungu entered the picture, playing the role of the 'good Samaritan' lawyer, and helping to put to bed a protracted matter that was becoming something of an albatross to successive governments. Lungu, working with colleague and buddy, Sakwiba Sikota, showed understanding and empathy for the Gabon families.

His quest to help them unlock the compensation money proved something of a balm to many of them. As he explained to them what was involved in getting the claims paid and how long the process could take, he would often find himself reaching for his own wallet to help because many of the claimants would have travelled from out of town with little by way of resources.

In an interview with this author, Kalusha explained that President Lungu that time, he was just a Lusaka lawyer and not the head of state, showed that he has a big heart. He worked diligently with others to get compensation for the bereaved families valued at billions of kwacha after that unfortunate disaster. 'It was a tough time for everyone, but President Lungu's role, even though no price can be placed on a lost life, was of such immense help to the families. The families themselves can attest to this. This, I believe, is one of the qualities that makes Lungu a unique man with a big heart.'

The whole process of resolving all the compensation claims took at least ten years and straddled two presidential terms (Frederick Chiluba and Levy Mwanawasa) before financial closure could be achieved. Kalusha, who was president of the FAZ when Zambia finally won a long overdue first Africa Cup title in 2012, coming almost as though by divine compensation, in Gabon. He had never worked with a better president than President Lungu.

'He (President Lungu) understands the importance of soccer and the role it plays in uniting Zambia,' Bwalya said. 'That is why I did not even hesitate to fully back him as the right candidate in the next polls.' Bwalya recalled that President Lungu had once said that he always prayed for a win for Zambia 'because when we (said President Lungu) win at soccer, Zambians unite across the religious and tribal divide'.

'I Am an Ordinary Man'

By October 2015, Edgar Lungu had held office as the sixth president of Zambia for a little over a year. Zambians and some people in the region had come to know him, or of him, in one measure or another, but not really know him in totality as no individual can really be known in that way, not even under the harshest public scrutiny as Lungu. But nevertheless about him, his constant public utterances, gestures of kindness, and even toughness were helping the Zambian public identify him with a certain character.

For instance, he was always at ease amongst children, wanting to hold them, he was at home amongst the common people as he made whistle-stops at open roadside markets during his country-wide tours and held simple conversation with them about the weather and even shared food with them. In addition, the local media, with all its ingenuity, also provided some sort of insight of who the man behind the man could be.

At one point, during a press conference as president, he cautioned his colleagues that 'I might speak with a soft voice, but I carry a big stick,' which meant he was not averse to taking touch action if a red flag was raised. At another media event, he threw a salvo at the opposition and nemesis, Guy Scott, just months ahead of the 2015 polls when asked if he was up to the election challenge by saying, 'What can you tell me about these guys (opposition and Guy Scott),' Lungu spoke off the script. 'I beat thumped them in the last elections (January 2015), and this time around, I will annihilate them and obliterate them permanently from the political market.'

But this interview Edgar Lungu had at Nkhwazi, the official residence on 10 October 2015 with the privately owned Hot FM, perhaps gave a further insight of the man. Below are some excerpt to President Lungu and his responses:

Q: How is it like being the president of Zambia?
A: It is a lonely job. You get blamed for a slump in copper prices, droughts and power cuts, and basically everything. But luckily for me, I am a people's man, nothing is insurmountable with corporation from a good team. The greatest challenge (in my job) is to get people to agree that you or to get people to be flexible, to lose some win some.

Q: How do people respond to some of your ideas?
You talk about a 2064 plan and people think you are crazy. You must plan ahead. My plan was that in 2021, President Michael Chilufya Sata's two terms would come to end office and we would go home, but here we are. I am president. Life is about accepting the dynamics as they come. When challenges come knocking, accept them and move on. I reflect a lot on where we are going (as president of Zambia, but I also get to spend a lot of time with my grandchildren whenever I have time. We (Esther and I) have six children, four girls two boys. They are adults with their own children. We have ten grandchildren.

Q: How's the PF as a party?
PF is a good example of a democratic party. If you recall how we tore each other after death of President Sata, but now we sit together? It is a marvel. We have lots of respect for one another. I don't regret coming in (as president) at a tough time (power shortages, fuel shortages, low copper prices, weak Kwacha). It's God's will, it's God's time. Nothing happens without God's intervention. I don't regret having come in at a bad time at all. I also think you can tell someone's worth as a leader depending on how they come out of a difficult time, or how they carry a nation during a tough time. I have been in office for nine months (as at time of interview), but I get the blame for things that figuratively happened or did not happen in 1964.

Q: Could Zambia have done better under previous leaderships?
I can only develop with the help of Zambians and the grace of God. We must have built on where KK left off. We should have done the same

thing from where FTJ left. But for some political reasons, their efforts were destroyed. Let's not mourn about the past, let us build on the present and learn from the past. I can't romanticise about the past KK days or the FTJ days. It (they) has their highs and lows. In my style of leadership, I want to ignore negative detractors. I want to concentrate on that which is progressive and uniting rather than that which slows us as a nation. I have no time for negativity. I want a unity of purpose and inclusiveness.

Q: Should you be re-elected in 2016?

2016 re-election is simple: continuity and stability. In the past, we lost out because people brought down everything built by previous administrations and started afresh. 2016 is about continuity and stability. Under Mwanawasa, things were even worse because he was rejected as an outsider given the manner he came in before he was later accepted. He was about to settle down, and he died unfortunately. RB took over, but before he could settle down, there was an election President Sata came in then he (Sata) died. If people are not of my ilk (if they don't share his vision), they could derail what we have started. We have, I have, walked the walk and talked the talk. We have a vision that is national in character. If I was not a national leader, for instance, I would have halted projects in areas where I was not voted for in 2015, but I have not and will not.

Q: Do you make time for ordinary people and officials?

I receive about fifty phone calls per minute on my mobile phone(s) alone, but I choose carefully which ones I have to take and listen carefully to once ones I pick up.

Q: Press conferences, Madam Inonge Wina abilities of work?

I have my own style as Edgar Lungu. I have a spokesman. He must talk on my behalf. I am not afraid of holding press conferences, but I want to give others chance to work too. Ministers etc. You want this President (Edgar Lungu) to talk about everything every day? I am very proud of my vice president, she is testimony of how skilled our women are in Zambia. Madam Inonge has wisdom due to her age and experience. She is not senile, age is but a number. Some people are old in age, but young and dynamic in mind. Others are young but mature in temperament.

Q: How do you take criticism of your leadership?

When you criticise me, it is like oil or ointment on my skin. I take it and rub it in and see what I can take on, or leave behind to make me a better leader. Some critics mean well. If you want this job (president's job), you have got to leave yourself open to criticism. You got to have a thick skin. It is not a job for the faint at heart.

Q: Nostalgia about the past as private citizen?

If you ask me once again, I can honestly tell you that I miss the great times I had with my friends back then. I wish I could be as free as I used to be while being president, but I can't. I miss you guys out there (laughs nostalgically).

Q: Declaration of National Day of Prayer, 18 October 2015, thoughts?

We (first family) have prayers in state house every Sunday just to avoid the hustle of a president driving out and disrupting traffic. 18 October was because I felt we, as a nation, as a people, were drifting away from the face of God by incessantly insulting each other, attacking each other, and so on. Apart from that, we have received so many hits on economic front, political front, and climatic front to an extent that I think we need divine intervention. We breathe because of God's grace. I am president because of God, so why not show gratitude to the creator? We should thank God when things are good, and pray to him when things are bad. I spoke to the nation and said please leave us alone if you don't believe in God. It is a personal decision based on faith, and I will not respond to it politically. Those that do not want to pray, please leave us alone with our God.

Q: Anti-Graft fight thoughts and reflections?

I despise corruption in all forms, but I am equally cautious that the fight against graft (in apparent reference to cartel days) has been used to victimise people in the past. I do not want a repeat of that. People lost entire incomes, jobs, etc., and had their names destroyed on the pretext of the fight against corruption. I don't want this victimisation to continue, not on my watch. I want justice and not vengeance. I don't want to be manipulated by those holier than though (ostensibly cartel) to punish their enemies or those they simply don't like. I have not stopped any investigations. I will, however, not be abused as president by special interest groups that want to punish their enemies, perceived, or real using the guise of graft. I don't want people to come and say 'can you investigate this guy?' Just because you don't like him. People punished in the past by so-called anti-corruption crusaders. Working under Mr Sata MHSRIP, I saw how this anti-corruption fight was used to punish innocent people. Unfortunately, in Zambia, when you become rich, you are corrupt. When you are old, you are a wizard. This has to change as we continue fighting the scourge of corruption.

Q: Firmness and fairness, are you firm enough? You have not fired people?
I am working with a team in all the areas. You need to trust the team you are working with in government, but you must supervise and not just delegate. Where people are not working, I will raise a red flag. It is like a football team. You have seen the referee, he warns players. It not about sacking (erring officers to be firm). I don't know why some Zambians are like this (enjoying misery of others). It's not about sacking. I don't know why some Zambians are so sadistic. They really love bloodletting, but that is not the way to go—at least that is not my way or style of doing things. I want justice. Even your child, when they (children) go wrong, you first wag your finger and say 'stop it boy'. Next, you give him a yellow card. Next, you give him the red card. You do that. If you are a responsible parent, you call in your child and seat him or her down and tell him or her to stop it. If he doesn't listen, then maybe you slap him, though now you cannot do that because of human rights (laughs good-heartedly). This is the same thing I do with my officials. I sit them down when there is a concern. I am afraid this call for blood (by some Zambians) is not good. If I have to sack people, there has to be a good reason. These are family men, these are good people whom I say work, and they have worked. They listen to me. Why should I sack them just to show that it is stylish for leaders to show that they have got clout (by sacking officials)? I will fire people, yes, I will shuffle people, yes, but it has to be within the best of intentions to bring out the best out of them, and not to deliberately punish them or simply to show them that I am the boss. They know I am the boss because I appointed them. When the time comes, I will sack people, but I will not do that to prove a point—to show that I am in charge. No, I won't do that. I am not a sadist.

Q: Legacy of ECL, what to live behind, he says 'I am no Superman.'
People should be leaders, people's power make people leaders. *The guy at the helm such as myself (the president) should be symbolic in nature. I would like to leave a legacy where the phantom called the president or the presidency is reduced to a human being occupying the office of the president on behalf of the people that entrusted him with that responsibility.* You see, my experience in this office of the president is that you are ring-fenced very quickly, isolated from the people, and they tell you what they (president's men) want you to hear. And in the process, you drift away from the people. You lose touch. The danger is before long, you are called names, and you are out of office. I want to meet as many people as possible while in office. I want to be remembered as an ordinary person who became president, a person who brought ordinary and human characteristics to the office of the presidency. Not where the president cannot go wrong, where the president is all powerful, where the president cannot fall ill, where the president cannot enjoy a game of soccer with friends and cheer and clap, where I cannot be a human being anymore because I am the president. No, I think it's not correct. I want people, Zambians, to begin seeing the president as one of them. Only difference is one of them is privileged to be at the helm. You see, there is certain protocols and traditions in the presidency, deeply imbedded that make you appear like you are the wisest, the most handsome, you name it. There is that built-in mechanism, but it is up to you to maintain your humanity and break these barriers and ensure that you remain touch with the people. The people must actually feel you are with them and not super human. You can make mistakes and people must feel they can volunteer counsel, and you can take that counsel. I want to be remembered as a president who remained a human being, an ordinary mortal who could make mistakes, who could listen to a voice out there. It is very easy to say *nshafyumfwe* ('I will have it my way' as translated from local Bemba language), but by doing that, ignoring advice, you are injuring those that elected you into office, and those people will want to pay you back at an appropriate time like an election. If a bricklayer is happy and can relate to me, I will be very happy than if the brick layer is scared of me and thinks I am a God. There is something in the presidency, which takes away certain elements of humanity in people and turns them into monsters. I want to maintain the humanity. *Mona ba president, kuti nalanda shani? (Look, it's the president. What am I going to say?)*

Q: Your views on tribe?

Politicians encourage tribalism more than anyone. We must fight this scourge. It can't take us anywhere, it can't help us, and examples abound on the continent on where tribe has divided a nation or nations.

End of interview.

At the end of the interview, many Zambians likened Lungu to the kid next door who left town, made it big abroad, and came back to share a cup of tea with them with no hung ups of self-importance. It further endeared him to the electorate and consolidated his stay in state house.

President Edgar Lungu is known to get out of his way to shake hands and share hugs with children because he loves them. President Lungu is captured here with young Lubinda Mukwita when he was Minister of Defence of Zambia in 2014.

President Edgar Lungu watches a military parade mounted in his honour when he was a guest of Uganda's President Yoweri Kaguta Museveni in Kampala, the capital of Uganda in October 2016.

President Edgar Lungu with President Museveni during a military parade in the Zambian leader's honour.

THE MINISTER OF DEFENCE

Notwithstanding the surprise element, if one were to be completely analytical, the Defence Ministry appointment couldn't have been that big a surprise for Lungu. Neither for that matter should it have been for anyone else who might have been paying attention to him in the past year or so. In his usual devil-may-care fashion, Sata had shown that Lungu was his blue-eyed boy, the one favoured above all, perhaps even the anointed one, should he for any reason have to leave state house. If Sata's decision to keep on loading Lungu with ever more responsibilities was not indicative enough of how highly he thought of Lungu, then the final pointer, surely, was that of his choice of person to act in his place whenever he would leave the country, as earlier discussed.

During his presidency, Sata frequently travelled outside the country, sometimes on official duty, and occasionally to seek medical attention abroad as his health continued to fail after a stroke he had suffered in the pre-2011 campaigns that left a mark on him. From the time Sata became the elected president of Zambia in 2011, the position of acting president rotated between then GBM, Finance Minister Alexander Bwalya Chikwanda aka ABC, Wynter Kabimba, and mostly, Edgar Lungu who served on at least three occasions. Interestingly, Vice President Guy Scott, who, under normal circumstances, should have been the one left to deputise, never served in this role while Sata was alive.

Anyway, by October 2014, the person left as acting president when President Sata left the station again was Edgar Lungu. As expected in public life, the special favour that Lungu enjoyed did not go down well in some quarters. Lungu's philosophical response to this was that in politics, just as in love and war, one could not attract as much attention as he was getting from Sata and not have some enemies.

Self-styled kingmakers, such as The Post newspaper, intensified its mission to destroy Lungu. The Post and rogue online media, at any given time, portrayed Lungu as a reckless and injudicious politician who could not possibly be taken seriously. Allegations linked Lungu's law firm to the misuse of clients' money. The message from The Post newspapers and online publications were essentially that Lungu should not be considered for high office, as he was neither competent nor trustworthy. None of the accusations against Lungu were substantiated of course, none at all, and no one complained of inefficiency at the Ministries of Home Affairs, Ministry of Justice, and Ministry of Defence to name but a few.

As for the misuse of clients' money, this was rather inconsistent with other accounts of Lungu's conduct, particularly when one considers the Gabon Disaster K16 billion. The amount of money was substantial, and the beneficiaries unsophisticated. However, those funds, as records show, were fully accounted for after the man did pro bono work.

The more the muck was raked against Lungu, the higher he seemed to rise. The section of the press not in Lungu's camp began to look like maybe they were trying a little too hard? Their bid to destroy public confidence in Lungu seemed to only serve as fuel for the Lungu to rise and gain public sympathy as the nice guy being mistrusted by the powerful. It was, in a sense, reminiscent of the biblical comparison of the stone that the builders had rejected turning out to be the chief cornerstone. Lungu was on his way up, and the negative publicity propelled him further. He was a man on fire.

But why was a section of the private media so hostile? Lungu's unpleasant interaction with the local media is strongly suspected to have originated from his solid anti-gay stance by a section of the private media that reportedly embraced gayism. The other was perhaps because he had shown open contempt for special interest groups or cartels that once were linked to run public office holders and held them at ransom.

Paramount among the reasons as later emerged is the cartel had candidates or a candidate it preferred, had an understanding with, and could work with for the greater control of the national wealth resources, Edgar Lungu, with his pro-poor and squeaky clean background that made him hard to blackmail, did not fit the space. He did not inspire the cartel that wanted power for a few and not for the many that Lungu openly spoke for and lived among in Chimwemwe and represented in Chawama.

Run-ins with the press were not the only source of disquiet for Lungu who, in fact, seemed to be quite the magnet for controversy at that time. For instance, while serving as Minister of Home Affairs, Lungu had denied former president, Rupiah Banda, passage abroad to South Africa on a planned medical check-up for the aging retired leader.

The reason Lungu advanced was that the former president, turned away at the international airport in Lusaka, might be a flight risk as he was being probed for corruption. Needless to say, it is under Lungu that RB's immunity against prosecution was lifted or restored.

This decision was highly debated in many quarters of Zambian society and soundly criticized, but Lungu stuck to his guns by law. Flight risk became a new word in Zambian political parlance, thanks to Lungu yet again. He already had, to his growing Lungu vocabulary 'you can't hunt with fox and play with hare', including 'let them have their say, we shall have our way', and if 'you rub me the wrong way, I will fall on you like a tonne of bricks'.

POWER EX-OFFICIO

As the person holding the positions of Minister of Defence, Minister of Justice, and secretary general of the ruling party, Lungu was arguably the most powerful man in the country, second only to the 'big man' himself. This was notwithstanding the fact that the second position, that is vice president, was officially in somebody else's name. Certainly, by the time of Sata's demise on 28 October 2014, Lungu was very powerful indeed. This was both, in fact, owing to the substantive title he was holding, and later on in essence after being obliged to surrender the acting president position to Guy Scott.

Lungu's dramatic rise to power, grappling with all the thorns that go with the rose on his way, has been nothing short of a fairy tale and is definitely unprecedented in Zambia's fifty years as a nation. His secret? Combining humility, perseverance, and a huge dose of patience into a deadly winning formula. Of course, Lungu was extensively helped by being in the right party at the right time; also the fact that he just so happened to be in the inner circle of a serving and popular president. At any rate, Edgar Lungu is bound to keep tongues wagging for a while to come, both in national and regional politics, with his humble but effective blend of politics.

By November 2014, it was increasingly apparent to a good number of Zambians just who was emerging as the front-runner for the office of the president of Zambia. Superstition and religious mumbo jumbo aside, most people were starting to accept that the mantle of leadership had, in reality, fallen on Lungu. It was to him that the baton had been handed by the departed president to complete the remaining one year and eight months of Sata's five-year term.

Following a narrow 48 per cent victory in the tightly fought January 2015 presidential poll, Lungu's task as a transitional leader was to get the PF, and especially himself, beyond the 2016 election. Following the January 2015 election victory, Lungu had said, 'I have gotten over the shock of the appointment, but I think I am equal to the task without bragging.' This was a typical Lungu response. It was perhaps also a fitting conclusion to a dizzying circuit in what some in the media have called the fastest heavily contested rise and rise in the modern history of Zambian politics.

The Zambian press were not the only ones excited by the dramatic events as they were unfolded ahead of Lungu's 2015 election. The international media, always keen watchers of Zambian politics, also acknowledged Lungu's spectacular rise from being, so to speak, a nobody—an ordinary guy.

Reuters described Lungu as a lawyer who had risen rapidly from backroom politics to being a fiery presidential front runner. Reuters described the Lungu ascension pace as breathtaking, unseen before in Zambia, save for Chiluba's rise to power in 1991, which in any case was a revolution. The agency described Lungu as having a 'steely determination that few knew lay beneath his quiet exterior'.

The SABC interviewed Lungu soon after his January 2015 victory regarding his 'winning formula'. Lungu summed up in three parts what he thought most accurately defined him as a politician: loyalty, patriotism, and respect for the hierarchy. 'I ran for parliament in Chawama in 2001 and lost. Later, someone else was chosen to run, and I supported the candidate but remained in the party.'

President Lungu's patience and loyalty, according to local pundits, is nothing short of extraordinary. To questions regarding his aspirations for the country, President Lungu maintains that he primarily wants to significantly reduce extreme poverty in Zambia. President Lungu also wants to be the man that helped Zambia diversify from the mono-economics of copper.

Lungu, according to some fellow lawyers that speak in confidentiality, was a totally different prospect from Sata as a potential leader. 'If you asked anyone six months ago (before 25 January 2015) who would be the next president of Zambia, no one would have picked Edgar,' a lawyer colleague told Reuters. 'That, in itself, was a strength because we', the lawyer said, 'should have known that he is a force. He is a quiet guy but very persuasive.'

'He's got this affable, laid-back style that makes people give him what he wants without realising they are giving him or without him even asking,' another lawyer said.

UNTO RANGER AND
TASILA LUNGU, A SON

The opening of the mines on Zambia's Copperbelt in the early 1900s precipitated one of the greatest rural–urban migration events in Africa. People came from all parts of the country (notably, Tanzania and Malawi) to seek paid employment in the mines and escape the uncertainties of a subsistence agricultural lifestyle.

Edgar Lungu's father, Ranger Padule Saili Lungu, was one such migrant, having originated from Mukwama Village in the Petauke District of the Eastern Province close to the border with Malawi. Together with his wife, Tasila Eliza Jere Lungu, the appropriately named Mr Ranger Lungu travelled some more than 800 kilometres from the Eastern to the Copperbelt Province. Not only was the Copperbelt a thriving commercial hub, it has also been the biggest tribal melting pot for most of Zambia's existence, as mine owners indiscriminately housed their workers together in mine townships.

And so it was that Nsenga speakers, like the Lungus, might find themselves neighbours with Tonga speakers on the left, Luvales on the right, and indeed Lozis in the middle. The different tribes had no choice but to get along, as their children played together, went to the same schools, and often intermarried. Divisions along tribal lines were thrown right out of the window, and this shaped Lungu's childhood to look beyond tribe and judge and treat people based on their abilities and human worth.

Edgar Lungu was born at Ndola Central Hospital on 11 November 1956 in very humble circumstances. His father worked (odd jobs) on the mines and the railways. Before then, he had worked for a Catholic priest (without education). His mother, like his father, had no formal education, but she worked hard selling vegetables and other odd stuff at the market to educate and feed Lungu and his siblings. Lungu was the third child out of a brood of seven.

The Lungu family moved to Kitwe when he was still a baby, taking up residence in the mining township of Chimwemwe where Daddy did odd jobs. For young Edgar, growing up in the rough Chimwemwe neighbourhood provided valuable life skills. Here, he not only picked up his fluent Bemba, but also learned grit and doggedness in holding down a resolve, and no doubt how to hold his own in a dog fight. These qualities were to serve him very well in later life.

Edgar's father, a mild-mannered man, passed on some important principles of his to his son. Edgar learned from his father the value of hard work, the importance of family, respect for elders, and the need to share whatever God blessed him with. It has also been said by those who knew the family well that Edgar most likely inherited his legendary generosity from his father. Lungu's mother was a woman possessed of grace and natural beauty. It is from her that Lungu got his fair complexion.

As Lungu recalls, 'We did not have much in terms of material (things) as a family; but whatever little we had was equally shared amongst all of us.' Lungu views those early lessons in 'sharing' as the basis of his magnanimous disposition, stating, 'Equitable distribution of resources started for me at a very tender age. I was taught to give more than I would expect to get.'

Edgar married Esther Nyawa Lungu thirty years ago as at 2016, and together, they have six children, who, in turn, have blessed them with ten grandchildren—some of whom help to occupy space at the big Nkwazi House with Grandpa Edgar and Grandma Esther.

Esther, who is a secretary by profession, epitomises the supportive and accommodating politician's wife. She long ago gave up her own career in order to support his career, to nurture their children, and to create a home environment to which Edgar could escape from the stress of court and boardrooms and, later on, the difficulties of a politician's life. Ever the keeper, Esther has uncomplainingly welcomed strangers, sometimes putting them up, and is often called upon to feed unexpected crowds who stream in and out of their home at awkward times even as a First Lady.

DADDY'S GIRL

There's always a child or two of the first family that goes on to make a public name for him or herself. A whole book could be written about the acts of the children of Zambia's successive first families. There have been the good, the bad, and the plain ugly.

Edgar Lungu has six children; among them Tasila, Daliso, Agness, Willie, and Chiyesu. While the rest seem happy keeping a low profile, Tasila is already carving a public profile for herself and serving as the public face of the family. She is councillor for Nkolomba Ward in her father's Chawama Constituency, having been elected to the seat in the election of 2016. She had been tipped for the post of deputy mayor, but then declined the invitation by sections of the party in Lusaka to go for it.

Tasila stole the media limelight shortly after her father took office as president of Zambia with her short natural hair and simple elegance, copied, as she says, from her grandmother who she credits with having raised her father to be the wonderful dad that he is. Spend the shortest while listening to Edgar talk to his daughter or vice versa, and it becomes obvious that Tasila is a real 'daddy's girl'. She says, like the other siblings, she enjoys a 'frank' relationship with their dad. She describes him as having 'a big, warm heart, and the simplest way to describe Dad is that he is an extremely loving and God-fearing man'.

Tasila was taught from an early age that success requires hard work and total dedication, and that she should follow her own path and dream big—words that have resonated with her throughout her working life. She recalls how in a recent heart to heart with her dad about her earlier career, she had wanted to quit and start a new chapter to follow her dream to promote entrepreneurship and innovation among the youth. The complication was that her dream would very likely not earn her much money in the short-term. This seemed at odds with her dad's earlier advice to her to never quit a job unless you have already found another one. Surprisingly, in this instance, her dad encouraged her to follow her heart, telling her, 'What is important is that you follow your passion and help people along the way. Money must never ever be the greatest motivation of your life.'

Tasila knew the depth of that last sentiment for, after many years of observing her father, she knew that 'people matter more than money to him'. She describes how Lungu loved his work, often putting in extra hour for little or no money. His greatest motivation? Probably the fact that Lungu hates to see people suffer, and will always go out of his way to help, says Tasila. 'Dad always tries to do the right thing, and I believe that his connection with his creator, the good Lord, is the source of his wisdom and compassion. He is simply the best Dad ever,' she says.

Tasila also describes a love for reading in her father and how, as a child, she was awed by his vast collection of books held in the wall-to-wall shelves in his study. The *Long Walk to Freedom* (on Nelson Mandela) was always a great favourite of Lungu's, and had pride of place on his desk right next to the Bible. That is why it was such a 'special treat' for Tasila when one day, her father picked up the Mandela biography and gave it to her. On the inside of the cover, in neat handwriting, Lungu wrote, 'To my daughter, Tasila, in recognition of your spiritual growth. Love, Dad.' That book is 'one of the best presents he has ever given me', Tasila says.

Other well-thumbed volumes are such inspirational works as the biography of Oprah Winfrey. Lungu also had, and still has, a great appetite for the *African Writers Series*, with classics such as Ferdinand Oyono's *House Boy* being one of his other favourites.

Another Lungu trait that is much talked about by all those acquainted with him is his generosity, with many describing him as a 'giver'.

There are two types of people in the world, there are 'givers' and then there are 'takers'. It is widely believed that 'givers' perform all sorts of selfless acts with no expectation of reciprocity. Lungu, in Tasila's eyes fits the 'giver' bill.

His wife, Esther, says Lungu can tirelessly pitch in for his colleagues, eagerly mentor underlings, and regularly prioritise other people's needs above his own. It is his nature, according to the first lady known as 'Queen Esther', for her own works of charity. The account is given by a young executive from Lungu's days as minister of home affairs, making the 'giver' image a very apt description of Lungu. Relating his first-hand experience of Lungu's generosity, the executive says, 'I know he would probably not like this repeated', and then goes on to tell how Honourable Lungu had, on several occasions, been more than generous to him, looking out for him as if he were his baby brother.

Once, when the young executive was going on a trip abroad, Honourable Lungu told him to go by his home saying, 'See Auntie Esther, she must give you something for a drink or meal while you're abroad.'

At the Lungu (off Brentwood Drive) residence, a beaming Mrs Lungu handed him an envelope saying, 'Your uncle asked me to give you this envelope for your trip just in case.' The envelope contained cash in crisp 100 US dollar bills.

Similar stories abound by other beneficiaries of Lungu's selfless giving in different situations, some whose university tuition fees he has quietly funded in endless and a well-known Lusaka orphanage whose fundraising efforts he has consistently supported.

While many have received cash, there are those who have benefitted through pro bono services, or been helped along by one of the many spontaneous acts of kindness that Lungu is well-known for. In response to the various sentiments of gratitude, Lungu says, 'I am not a wealthy man. But if I have something that can be shared amongst friends who have less than I do, I see no reason why I shouldn't share it because I also have been lucky, and been given things in life.'

President Edgar Lungu with his daughter, Tasila Lungu who has decided to walk the political path like her father, the sixth President of Zambia.

President Edgar Lungu captured deep in prayer. The Zambian President, a practicing Christian has since he assumed office declared 18th October a National Day of Prayer. President Lungu has also contributed personal financial resources to the construction of an inter-denominational House of Prayer in Lusaka because the Cathedral of the Holy Cross is no longer huge enough to accommodate a growing number of population during national prayer functions.

President Edgar Lungu with his spouse of more than 30 years Esther Nyawa Lungu as a young couple before the dream of becoming a President and a First Lady was even hatched.

President Edgar Lungu shares a light moment with the Holy Father Pope Francis during his unprecedented trip of the Holy See in February 2016. President Lungu became the first and only Zambian President to receive a papal invitation to the Holy See.

-"Walking the walk and talking the talk. President Edgar Lungu is flanked by senior diplomat and author Anthony Mukwita in sun glasses while Special Assistant for Politics Kaizar Zulu on the left and Special Assistant for press and PR Amos Chanda listen on during State House golfing event in August 2015.

Lessons from the Campaign Trail

On the arduous campaign trail leading up to January 2015, Lungu had to draw on his large reservoir of internal strength, grit, and stamina, but especially, self-belief. By polling day, Lungu was mentally, physically, and emotionally drained, not to mention the effect on his pocket and the wallets of those close to him. Lungu had to reach deep into his spiritual side, saying, 'I know that there is God for us all up there. If you believe in him like I do, he will give you glory.' He openly proclaimed this.

He was also greatly inspired by the account of Mandela's journey and how he overcame the near-impossible odds under South Africa's brutal segregationist system to become the first black president of post-apartheid South Africa. But Lungu had local heroes too, one of whom is Zambia's first president, Kenneth Kaunda, from whom he has learned a great deal about perseverance in sticking to one's ideology.

Borrowing from one of Mandela's numerous lines, Lungu would say, 'I am fundamentally an optimist. Whether that comes from nature or nurture, I cannot say. Part of being optimistic is keeping one's head pointed toward the sun and one's feet moving forward. At least that is what the great Nelson Mandela taught us.'

Lungu admits that there were many dark moments when his faith in humanity and the political system was sorely tested, 'But I would not, and could not, give myself up to despair. That way (lurked) defeat and death.' Given the circumstances, one could say Lungu's favourite past-time (he is a practised quotematic) did a lot to keep him going during those dark uncertain days.

Lungu also displayed a great sense of humour during some of those dark moments. While his captive audience mulled over his deep thought and hung on to his every word, he would quickly jog their minds back to reality: 'The thoughts, gentlemen, that was the great Nelson Mandela from whose wisdom we keep learning. They are not mine.'

Much like a sage sharing a moment of introspection with his closest students, Lungu would explain during private moments his deep hatred of such vices as tribalism. He saw tribalism as a form of apartheid with individuals preferring members of their own tribe whether or not they were competent. This can be deadly when it became the basis of social, political, and economic interaction. Lungu would talk at length about his deep desire to rid the nation, especially institutions, of this narrow-minded vice.

Following his victory at the polls, Lungu confessed to having learned a valuable lesson once he had endeavoured to run for high office, saying, 'I was so naïve about the regional and tribal pattern of Zambian politics, which I think is just plain wrong,' Lungu said after his victory, praising former President Kenneth Kaunda's vision of 'One Zambia One Nation!'

For his part, Lungu describes himself as Zambian by tribe, saying, 'Tribalism is bad, gentlemen. It punishes and discriminates the innocent. It has no place in our new Zambia.' During his presidential campaign, Lungu did his best to dismantle the tribal card, preaching unity of purpose, which he said was what would eventually build Zambia. Someone has likened Lungu's approach to the tribal question, to that of the celebrated neurosurgeon, Ben Carson's, approach to the 'race' issue in the USA. During an interview on Fox Television during the run-up to the primaries in the 2016 election, the inevitable question came up why he never spoke about race despite his being of African American origin. Carson told the interviewer, 'I operate on that, which defines us and not skin (colour).'

Once on the porch of his ministerial house during one of the many tribal debates, children of his friends that had come visiting played with his grandson, Lishomwa. Randomly, in trying to make a practical example against the evil of tribalism, he called one of the children whom he regarded as just another grandson. 'Lubinda, please come over here, son. *Muzuhile cwani?*' (Which is Lozi from Western Province, and is a common greeting literally translated as 'good day or how are you?') Cleary flabbergasted, the child, Lubinda, said with a smile, 'I have no idea what you are talking about.'

Lungu then turned to his captive audience to make a point. 'You see, that child, he is not Lozi. He is not Bemba. He is a Zambian, and it would be wrong to punish him because his father is Lozi or some such.' Looking ahead to the 2016 elections, Lungu said, 'We will campaign from the word go by our deeds. Africa is full of examples of people who have done great deeds such as Dr Kenneth Kaunda. He inspires me.'

LUNGU, BRIEF POLITICAL HISTORY

Edgar Lungu started in the PF Government as a junior minister in the office of the vice president in 2011. The following year, he was elevated to minister of home affairs. Edgar was appointed minister of defence in October 2014. Sata, his health failing, had Lungu recalled from a trip to Angola to act as president, while he went away for medical treatment. President Sata subsequently died on that trip on 28 October 2014 in a West London hospital.

Quick Edgar Lungu Facts

- 13 September 2016 Edgar Chagwa Lungu is sworn in as sixth President of the republic of Zambia for the second time
- 25 January 2015, Edgar Lungu first wins the tightly contested presidential poll after the death of Sata
- 11 November 1956, Edgar Lungu is born in Ndola Central Hospital
- Wifes name, Esther Nyawa Lungu
- Fathers name, Ranger Padule Saili Lungu
- Mothers name Tasila Eliza Jere Lungu
- Children: Janet, Agnes, Willie, Tasila, Daliso and Chiyeso
- Home town: Chimweme Township in Kitwe
- High school name: Mukuba High School in Kitwe, copperbelt province
- Higher education: University of Zambia graduated on 17-10-81
- Past positions: minister of home affairs, minister of justice, secretary general of the ruling PF, chair of PF disciplinary committee, president of all African parties, deputy minister in the office of the vice president and president of PF.

Milestones as President of Zambia

- Infrastructure roll out of roads, bridges, universities, and airports
- Signing of a new constitution that allows dual citizenship and 50 per cent plus one in 2015
- Reaffirming Zambia as a Christian nation and turning to God every time there is a national challenge
- Open and public rejection of tribalism and embracing Christianity as a core value

REFLECTIONS

Presidential elections were held on 11 August 2016 in Zambia, for the second time in twenty months, and after the ensuing post–election drama. Edgar Lungu has emerged the winner, proving to the country and the subregion at large that he was not the political lightweight that some might have thought him to be.

There were many who had attributed his triumph in 2015 to a sympathy vote, having stood to replace the popular and charismatic, Michael Sata, who had died just three years into his first term in office after several attempts.

No such doubts about the 2016 victory. Edgar Lungu had stood and won as his own man. His inauguration was attended by the good and great of African politics. Among them were Botswana's General Ian Khama, Robert Mugabe of Zimbabwe, and Tanzanian first female vice president, Samia Suluhu Hassan to represent His Excellency John Magufuli. President Uhuru Kenyatta of Kenya was represented by Vice President William Ruto.

The long list of endorsements and well-wishers included the US State Department, the Carter Centre, and—in his own personal capacity— US President Barak Obama. The *Book of Congratulations* bulged with endorsements and best wishes from across the globe.

Shortly after his swearing-in on 13 September, Lungu got on with the arduous task of putting together his cabinet. He began by shortlisting heads of some key ministries needed to hold the government together, while he headed for the United Nations General Assembly in New York beginning 22 September. With vice president, Mrs Inonge Wina, to stand in as acting president, Lungu had only to put in place a few more appointments to ensure the country remained governable in his absence.

His first batch of ministers came as a surprise to many. The influential ministry of finance position went to Felix Mutati, putative leader of Zambia's third largest party, the MMD. Further surprises were in the offing as he handed the Ministry of National Planning to Lucky Mulusa and Ministry of Agriculture to Dora Siliya, both from the MMD—the latter having served in a previous cabinet under Rupiah Banda.

With these surprise appointments, Lungu had once again proved himself hard to anticipate. Both friends and foes were left wondering what game the president was playing. No doubt these were competent appointees, but was there more to it? Was Lungu trying to outfox the opposition by bringing his friends close and enemies even closer?

Further, was there a message being sent out other than the president having openly stated that newcomers were welcome to the PF as the party metamorphosed into a party for all Zambians.

More pointedly, what impact would his actions have on his own rank and file in the PF? Quite a few of these faithful members would have believed themselves well-qualified and more deserving of the plum jobs being given to 'outsiders'. Would they desert the party on grounds of having been slighted, or would they retain confidence in their General, trusting his judgment as to which soldier could best handle what weapon for the greater good of the nation?

Lungu's re-election in 2016 was achieved against a background of economic challenges, including a global slump in commodity prices, resulting in lower earnings for the country's copper-export dependent economy, soaring national inflation, as well as a declining GDP. To compound issues, the country has, for the past three years, been experiencing a climate change induced power deficit resulting in highly inconvenient rationing (load-shedding), affecting both households and the wheels of the economy.

Clearly, the Edgar Lungu of 2016, with a full five-year term ahead of him and not the transitional one year, eight months of his previous mandate, will be an interesting man to watch. The 2016 election was significant in the sense that Lungu was able to finally put to rest the looming shadow of his predecessor and prove his own competence, as it were. Meanwhile, the world is watching to see what sort of president the humble lawyer from Chimwemwe and Chawama will prove to be, to see what legacy their president will carve for himself.

It was deeply hearing the president-elect, with deep sincerity, shout Founding President Kenneth Kaunda's rallying cry to Zambia's citizens: 'One Zambia, One Nation!' This being his opening statement in his first address to the crowds that had thronged state house to congratulate him, immediately after he was declared winner, it would seem that bringing unity to the nation is priority number one in President Edgar Lungu's mind. Needless to say, if anyone was in any doubt that Edgar Lungu could take tough decisions even if they affected those in his inner circle, the so-called untouchables, they were wrong.

He had once said, 'I may speak with a soft voice, but I carry a huge stick.'

Lungu proved his stick was huge indeed when, at a spur of a moment, he sacked Chishimba Kambwili, the gang ho minister of information and chief government spokesman, amidst accusations of graft. A new Lungu was now in charge.

It was going to be a long and interesting five years of the Edgar Lungu presidency.

AUTHOR'S NOTES

I first cut my teeth as a writer at a privately owned newspaper called The Sun in Lusaka, Zambia in 1993 before going international. Internationally, I corresponded for influential outlets such as *Bloomberg News*, the *Independent Foreign Service, Los Angeles Times* and *The New African* magazine, to mention but a few.

It was not, however, until October 2011 that I got my first public recognition as a writer. I was awarded the Best Investigative Journalism Award in a tightly contested World Bank Zambia sponsored competition. The award saw me get attached to the prestigious London-based Bureau of Investigative Journalism (BIJ) located at City University for a quarter of a year in the summer of 2012.

Earlier in 1994, I was privileged to have had a similar experience as the BIJ, except this was in the United States of America where I traversed various states including the nation's capital on what is called the international Visitor Leadership Programme or IVLP designed by the Department of State for future leaders in different fields.

By the time I was writing the book, I had already completed a Master of Professional Communication degree (MPC) by course work from Edith Cowan University in Western Australia. I earned six distinctions. Before becoming a diplomat, I worked as Deputy Managing Director, and later, Managing Director of the Zambia Daily Mail, the largest circulated daily newspaper in Zambia whose increase in sales I helped achieve. In fact the current Berliner shape of the newspaper was my personal idea as Managing Director.

I had already had occasion and honour to know President Edgar Chagwa Lungu at a personal level the time he was a young, fiery, and ambitious lawyer at Andre Masiye Law Firm. I was a rookie reporter then. I followed President Lungu's public law career from the time he represented the victims of the fated Gabon plane crash that killed thirty people to the time he first contested and lost a parliamentary seat in Chawama.

I, nevertheless, came to know President Lungu more closely when he was the understated, but ever so jovial and confident deputy minister in the office of the vice president in 2011, as well as legislator for Chawama. Because of his ever-disarming humbling demeanour, I took an interest in profiling him since there was little or no extensive written information on him as a lawyer or politician.

My writer's instinct told me a man with this level of humility and tenacity was a man to watch closely. I was right.

While I was in London at the BIJ in 2012, Hon. Lungu was no longer a deputy minister in the office of the vice president. He was promoted to position of minister of home affairs, a very influential cabinet position. He would be in charge of homeland security among other duties.

Mr Lungu's quick rise to political office and the unfortunate twist of fate that saw President Michael Sata die, in some part, inspired this book. This is not to mention the many hats Lungu wore before becoming president, defence minister, minister of justice, and secretary general of the ruling PF, etc.

Taking advantage of an immense lack of dependable and verifiable data for people to base their decisions on regarding the rising political star that was Lungu, now running for President of Zambia, I penned a booklet that attempted to explain who Edgar Lungu was in a few chapters. It was an instant hit and was reproduced word for word in local media when he became president. I knew then, as I know now, that people would never tire from wanting to read more about this 'ordinary man' that became president of Zambia.

The story I tell is based on my own experience, observations, and interviews with those that like and dislike President Lungu. Newspaper story reviews and heart to heart discussions between the president and myself form a huge component of the book too. It is a story aimed at pushing Zambia more onto the global village via literature using an ordinary man who achieved extraordinary things.

Zambia is already traditionally known as Africa's haven of peace, and my thought is that projecting it through a national leader with feet on the ground would help add value and bring continental and even global attention to this great nation. On record, Zambia remains the most peaceful country in Africa that has never been to war since independence in 1964.

I spoke intensely and regularly with President Lungu in order to clarify some things, and at all the time, day or night, he never tired to lend me his ear, and his patience is something of special note for a man like the proverbial or mythical Atlas carries the weight of Zambia on his shoulders at the edge of Gaia.

I hope my book helps add value to the body of knowledge literature in Zambia. If it inspires fellow writers to produce their take on the country, or on President Lungu and other national icons, even better.

I thank a number or people, perhaps too numerous to mention, for encouraging me during this arduous and sometimes scary project. President Edgar Lungu and First Lady Esther top the list.

My wife Elaine here in Stockholm, Sweden and my sons, Lubinda and Lushomo, cannot be forgotten. I thank them for tolerating my mood swings as I burnt the midnight oil in order to get the project on the shelf. I also thank Mr Gerald Mulwanda whom I engaged to edit my manuscript. You are a great Editor Gerald, mazel tov.

I cannot thank enough my lawyers, Mr Lewis Chisanga Mosho of Lewis Nathan and Company, for the legal audit his team undertook on the book.

My mother in Livingstone, Elizabeth Mukwita, cannot be left out of the list of people to thank while I know that my late father, Mr Frederick Lubinda Mukwita, a former university lecturer and teacher of English, would have offered the best critic for my work had he been around. My whole family is thanked.

Special thanks go to the State House Press Office team led by Amos Chanda, the president's spokesman at the time of writing this book, and State House photographers, Eddie Mwanaleza, Thomas Nsama, and Salim Henry. I thank Mr Mwanaleza, especially, for providing the cover picture and many others at a snap of a finger during the project.

The following are some of the publications I have referenced some of the material from contained in the book: The Daily Nation of Zambia, Zambia Daily Mail, Times of Zambia, ZNBCTV, MuviTV, Radio Phoenix, and Hot FM. This includes interviews I had with colleagues that worked close to the Lungu office, and of course, the first lady, Mrs Esther Nyawa Lungu, who gave me a rare insight of Edgar Lungu, a husband, grandparent, and partner.

If I have omitted anyone on the list of those I thank or learnt from, it is not by intention but by error. I hope you all enjoy reading this book as much as I enjoyed writing it. God bless you all.

A. L. M.

SUNDAY MAIL

NEWS:
ECZ wants law against wet season elections/2

PHOTO FOCUS:
Edgar wins as 6th President/4

IN-DEPTH:
Devastating impact of litter on environment/6

SPORTS:
Cape Verde warns Zambia /20

VOL 21 NO. 04 | JANUARY 25, 2015 | **WITHOUT FEAR OR FAVOUR** | www.daily-mail.co.zm | @zodomo24 ZAMBIA_DAILY_MAIL | PRICE: K4

EDGAR LUNGU IS PRESIDENT

ECZ dismisses HH's manipulation allegations

CHRISTINE CHISHA, MUNDE ZULU
Lusaka

UNITED Party for National Development (UPND) leader Hakainde Hichilema says he will not concede defeat accusing the Electoral Commission of Zambia (ECZ) of manipulating votes.

Continues on Page 3

■ **Chief Justice declares PF candidate duly-elected**

ANGELA CHISHIMBA, YANDE SYAMPEYO
Lusaka

EDGAR Chagwa Lungu is Zambia's sixth republican President, after being declared winner of a tight election contest last night.

The lawyer-cum-politician, contesting on a Patriotic Front (PF) ticket, succeeds the late President Michael Sata who died in October last year, after an election widely commended as free and fair.

Mr Lungu emerged victorious with 807,925 votes representing 48.33 percent of votes cast, relegating his closest rival Hakainde Hichilema of the United Party for National Development (UPND) into second place on 780,168 (46.67 percent).

Returning Officer Justice Lombe Chibesakunda declared Mr Lungu winner at Mulungushi International Conference Centre at 22:30 hours in Lusaka yesterday, sending PF members into jubilation.

Continues on Page 3

EL to be sworn in

NOMSA NKANA
Lusaka

ALL IS set for the inauguration ceremony of Zambia's sixth President, Edgar Lungu, at the National Heroes Stadium in Lusaka today.

Secretary to the Cabinet Roland Msiska said in a statement that the ceremony will start at 19:00 hours to be followed by a luncheon to be hosted at State House at 14:00 hours.

"All dignitaries to the inauguration ceremony and the State luncheon should hold their invitations which were proposed for yesterday Saturday January 24 as valid," Dr Msiska said.

He said access by dignitaries to the National Heroes Stadium will be by invitation while designated wings on the centre, southern and northern parts of the stadium will be open to the public without invitations.

Continues on Page 3

Stakeholders congratulate Lungu

(Full story on Page 3)

ZAMBIA'S Sixth Republican President, Edgar Chagwa Lungu at his home in Lusaka after he was declared winner of the election last night.
PICTURE: SALIM HENERY/SHENPA

Poll results at a glance

Name	Party	votes	% votes
Edgar Lungu	PF	807,925	48.33
Hakainde Hichilema	UPND	780,168	46.67
Edith Nawakwi	FDD	15,321	0.92
Nevers Mumba	MMD	14,609	0.87
Tilyenji Kaunda	UNIP	9,737	0.58
Eric Chanda	4R	8,054	0.48
Elias Chipimo	NAREP	6,002	0.36
Godfrey Miyanda	HP	5,757	0.34
Dan Pule	CDP	3,293	0.20
Ludwig Sondashi	FDA	2,073	0.12
Peter Sinkamba	GPZ	1,410	0.08

TOTAL VOTES CAST 1,671,662
AVERAGE VOTER TURNOUT 32.36

■ **Mugabe in for inauguration**

ZIMBABWEAN President Robert Mugabe has arrived in Zambia for the inauguration ceremony of Zambia's 6th President, Mr Edgar Lungu today.

Minister of Foreign Affairs Harry Kalaba said Mr Mugabe arrived in the country on Friday.

Mr Mugabe is among three heads of state expected to attend the inauguration. Other dignitaries already in the country for the inauguration include

the prime ministers of Swaziland and Tanzania.

"Others who are expected are presidents Hifikepunye Pohamba of Namibia, Joseph Kabila of the Democratic Republic of Congo (DRC), several ministers of foreign affairs Ministers representing their heads of governments, and the diplomatic corps among others." he said.
NOMSA NKANA
Lusaka

■ **Police beef up security**

MORE Police officers will be deployed today to provide security from the Mulungushi International Conference Centre up to National Heroes Stadium in Lusaka, the venue for the inauguration ceremony for Zambia's Sixth President.

Police spokesperson Charity Munganga-Chanda said in an interview that traffic officers will monitor the flow of traffic in Lusaka city.

"We are therefore appealing to motorists

to follow traffic rules and regulations even while they are celebrating. They all need to be sober-minded because as police we remain vigilant and we will arrest anybody found wanting," she said.

Ms Chanda also appealed to political party leaders to restrain their cadres from engaging in any activities that might disturb the peace in the country.
SYLVESTER CHISHIMBA
Lusaka

■ **Chipimo snr gets national funeral**

SECRETARY to the Cabinet Roland Msiska has announced that declared tomorrow, as a day of national mourning for former Lusaka Minister and Ambassador Elias Chipimo Senior, who died on January 18, in South Africa.

Dr Msiska said in a statement released in Lusaka yesterday that national mourning will be observed on the day of burial from

06:00 hours to 18:00 hours.

He said flags will fly at half mast and activities of entertainment nature postponed or cancelled.

Dr Msiska said Mr Chipimo's burial will be held at his farm at plot number 487 A off Leopards Hill road in Lusaka after a requiem mass to be held at 11:00hours.
SYLVESTER CHISHIMBA
Lusaka

ZAMBIA AT A GLANCE - POLITICAL TIMELINE

| COUNTRY: | ZAMBIA |
| Capital: | LUSAKA |

- Became capital (Lusaka) of Northern Rhodesia in 1935
- Capital of independent Zambia from 1964
- Mushroomed in the 1960s
- Population: 1 million

2016 August 11	Zambia goes to Presidential and parliamentary elections
2016 August 15	Electoral Commission Zambia declares Edgar Chagwa Lungu victorious in the election
2016 August 16	UPND petitions presidential election results
2016 September 5	Constitution Court dismisses UPND electoral petition against Edgar Lungu
2016 September 13	Edgar Chagwa Lungu is sworn in as Zambia sixth President of before a capacity crowd in the National Heroes Stadium.

ZAMBIA AT A GLANCE - POLITICAL TIMELINE

16th Century	Arrival of peoples from Luba and Lunda empires of Zaire to set up small kingdoms. Zaire is currently the Democratic Republic of Congo lying on the northern border of Zambia.
Late18th Century	Portuguese explorers visit.
19th Century	Instability generated by migration as well as slave-trading by Portuguese and Arabs.
1851	British missionary David Livingstone visits.
COPPER DISCOVERED	
1889	Britain establishes control over Northern Rhodesia, administering the area using a system of indirect rule which leaves power in the hands of local rulers.
Late **1920s**	Discovery of copper, which later encourages an influx of European technicians and administrators.
1953	Creation of the Federation of Rhodesia and Nyasaland, comprising Northern Rhodesia, Southern Rhodesia (now Zimbabwe) and Nyasaland (now Malawi).
1960	UNIP (United National Independence Party) formed by Kenneth Kaunda to campaign for independence and dissolution of federation dominated by white-ruled Southern Rhodesia.
1963	Federation dissolved.
1964	Independence, with Kaunda as president.
Late 1960s-**70s**	Key enterprises nationalised. Private land nationalised in an unsuccessful agricultural improvement programme.
1972	Zambia becomes a one-party state, with UNIP as the only legal party.
HELP FOR REBELS	
1975	Tan-Zam railway opened, providing a link between the Copperbelt to the Tanzanian port of Dar es Salaam, reducing Zambian dependence on Rhodesia and South Africa for its exports.
1976	Zambia declares support for the independence struggle in Rhodesia. Zambian help proves crucial to the transition of Rhodesia to an independent Zimbabwe.
1990	Food riots.
1991	Multi-party constitution adopted. Movement for Multi-party Democracy (MMD) wins elections and its leader, Frederick Chiluba, becomes president.

ZAMBIA AT A GLANCE - POLITICAL TIMELINE

1996	Change to constitution effectively barring Kaunda from future elections. Chiluba re-elected.
1997	Attempted coup.
1999	A high court sentences 59 soldiers to death after they are found guilty of treason for the failed coup attempt in 1997.
2000 May	Fighting between Angolan forces and UNITA rebels spills over into Zambian territory.
2000 July	Environment Minister Ben Mwila expelled from the MMD and dropped from the cabinet after announcing his intention to run for president in 2001.
2000 December	UN officials estimate that up to 60,000 refugees fleeing fighting in the Democratic Republic of Congo move to Zambia in less than a week.

CHILUBA TROUBLE

2001 May	Setback for governing Movement for Multi-party Democracy as senior members hive off to create Forum for Democracy and Development. They're opposed to Chiluba's bid for a third term in office.
2001 July	Paul Tembo, former campaign manager for Chiluba who joined the opposition, is murdered shortly before he is due to testify against three ministers in a high-level corruption case.
2001 July	Zambia appeals for aid to feed some 2 million people after poor harvests caused by floods and drought.
2001 July	Final summit of the Organisation of African Unity (OAU), launch of the African Union.
	Image copyright AFP Image caption Levy Mwanawasa (l) succeeded Frederick Chiluba as president
2002 January	Levy Mwanawasa is sworn in as president amid opposition protests over alleged fraud in December's presidential elections.
2002 July	Parliament votes to remove ex-president Frederick Chiluba's immunity from prosecution.
2002 October	Government says it will not accept genetically modified (GM) maize to help alleviate the severe food shortages facing three million people.
2003 February onwards	Former president Frederick Chiluba is arrested and charged with corruption. Subsequent long-running trials are dogged by adjournments and procedural problems.

ZAMBIA AT A GLANCE - **POLITICAL TIMELINE**

2003 December	Supreme Court confirms death sentences on 44 soldiers for their role in 1997's failed coup; sentences are later commuted by President Mwanawasa.
2004 September	Many charges of corruption against former president Frederick Chiluba are dropped, but within hours he is re-arrested on six new charges.
2005 February	Supreme Court rejects opposition challenge to President Mwanawasa's 2001 election victory, but says ballot had flaws.
DEBT RELIEF	
2005 April	World Bank approves $3.8 billion debt relief package which will write off more than 50% of Zambia's debt.
	Around 50 workers killed in explosion at Chinese-owned explosives factory.
2005 November	President Mwanawasa declares a national disaster and appeals for food aid. He says more than a million Zambians face food shortages owing to drought.
2006 April	President Mwanawasa suffers a minor stroke. He resumes "light duties" after some weeks and later declares himself fit to run for re-election towards the end of the year.
2006 September	President Mwanawasa wins a second term.
2006 October	President announces discovery of oil in the west.
2007 January	Government launches economic recovery plan which envisages encouraging foreign investment.
2007 February	Chinese President Hu Jintao inaugurates a huge mining investment zone at the end of a two-day visit. His itinerary is cut short due to planned protests against the alleged exploitation of local workers by Chinese firms.
2007 May	The High Court in Britain rules that former president Frederick Chiluba and four of his aides conspired to rob Zambia of about $46 million.
2008 August	President Levy Mwanawasa dies, 59, in a Paris hospital, where he was being treated for the effects of a stroke in June.
2008 November	Vice-President Rupiah Banda sworn in as president after a narrow election win over the main opposition candidate, Michael Sata, who alleged fraud.
2009 August	Ex-President Chiluba is cleared of corruption after a six-year trial. The head of the anti-corruption task force is sacked after initiating an appeal against Chiluba's acquittal.

ZAMBIA AT A GLANCE - POLITICAL TIMELINE

2010 February	Zambia and China sign mining cooperation agreement and deal to set up joint economic zone.
	Supreme Court dismisses application by ex-President Chiluba aimed at preventing government from applying British High Court judgment convicting him of defrauding Zambia of $46m dollars.
2010 August	Zambia, China agree to build a second hydroelectric power plant on the Kafue River.
2010 October	Chinese mine managers charged with attempted murder following a multiple shooting at a mine where workers were demonstrating against conditions.
2011 January	Deadly clashes between police and demonstrators agitating for secession of western Zambia, known as Barotseland.
2011 June	Former President Frederick Chiluba dies.
CHANGE OF GOVERNMENT	
2011 September	Michael Sata becomes president.
2012 August	Chinese mine manager killed during pay protest.
2013 February	The government takes over the Chinese-owned Collum Coal mine after revoking its licence because of safety lapses.
2013 March	Former president Rupiah Bwezani Banda is charged with abuse of power shortly after being stripped of immunity by parliament.
2014 January	Opposition politician Frank Bwalya is charged with defamation after comparing President Sata to a potato in a radio interview.
2014 June	President Sata goes to Israeli on a "working holiday" amid rumours about his health.
2014 October 28	President Sata dies.
2015 January 25	Edgar Lungu becomes president after winning election.
2016 April	Rioting and looting following accusations that Rwandans who have fled to Zambia have been involved in ritual killings. President Lungu speaks of his country's collective shame over mob attacks on foreigners.

COMPILED AND RESEARCHED: Anthony Mukwita
LAYOUT AND DESIGN: Masuzgo Mtawali

2015 PRESIDENTIAL ELECTION RESULTS

	CANDIDATE NAME	PARTY	VOTES
	LUNGU, Edgar C	PF	807,925
	HICHILEMA, Hakainde	UPND	780,168
	NAWAKWI, Edith Z	FDD	15,321
	MUMBA, Nevers S	MMD	14,609
	KAUNDA, Tilyenji C	UNIP	9,737
	CHANDA, Eric M	4R	8,054
	CHIPIMO, Elias C M	NAREP	6,002
	MIYANDA, Godfrey K	HERITAGE	5,757
	PULE, Daniel M	CDP	3,293
	SONDASHI, Ludwig S	FDA	2,073
	SINKAMBA, Peter C	GREENS	1,410

TOTAL REGISTERED VOTERS
5,166,084

TOTAL VOTES CAST 1,671,662

TOTAL VOTES REJECTED
17,313

TURNOUT
32.36%

2016 PRESIDENTIAL ELECTION RESULTS

	Candidate Name	Party	Votes
	LUNGU, Edgar C	PF	1,860,877
	HICHILEMA, Hakainde	UPND	1,760,347
	NAWAKWI, Edith Z	FDD	24,149
	BANDA, Andyford M	PAC	15,791
	KABIMBA, Wynter M	RAINBOW	9,504
	CHISHIMBA, Saviour	UPP	9,221
	KAUNDA, Tilyenji C	UNIP	8,928
	SINKAMBA, Peter C	GREENS	4,515
	MWAMBA, Maxwell	DA	2,378

TOTAL REGISTERED VOTERS
6,698,372

TOTAL VOTES CAST 3,781,505

TOTAL VOTES REJECTED
85,795

TURNOUT
56.45%

Lightning Source UK Ltd.
Milton Keynes UK
UKOW02f0602280217
295467UK00002B/57/P